BY MARGE EDIE

BARGELLO QUILTS

That Patchwork Place®

Credits

Editor-in-Chief .... Barbara Weiland
Technical Editor .... Laura M. Reinstatler
Managing Editor .... Greg Sharp
Copy Editor .... Liz McGehee
Proofreader .... Leslie Phillips, Tina Cook
Design Director .... Judy Petry
Book Design .... David Chrisman
Cover Design .... Chris Christiansen
Photography .... Brent Kane
Illustration .... Brian Metz

Bargello Quilts©
© 1994 by Marge Edie
That Patchwork Place, Inc.,
PO Box 118, Bothell, WA 98041-0118 USA

That Patchwork Place®

Mission Statement

WE ARE DEDICATED TO PROVIDING QUALITY PRODUCTS THAT ENCOURAGE CREATIVITY AND PROMOTE SELF-ESTEEM IN OUR CUSTOMERS AND OUR EMPLOYEES.

WE STRIVE TO MAKE A DIFFERENCE IN THE LIVES WE TOUCH

That Patchwork Place is an employee-owned, financially secure company.

Printed in South Korea
99 98 97   6

Library of Congress Cataloging-in-Publication Data
Edie, Marge
      Bargello quilts / Marge Edie.
            p.   cm.
      ISBN 1-56477-067-2 :
      1. Strip quilting—Patterns. 2. Patchwork—Patterns.
   3. Patchwork quilts. I. Title.
TT835. E375   1994
746.46—dc20
                                        94-18419
                                        CIP

Preface and Acknowledgments

In October of 1990, Jennifer Amor came to our Lake and Mountain Quilters Guild to teach a Saturday workshop on creating a Bargello vest. Although various family obligations prevented me from attending the workshop, I did stop by long enough to become interested in the beauty of the techniques she was presenting. By Christmas, I had five Bargello lap throws in the mail for family members and was hooked on the Quilt-As-You-Build-It process!

"To the Sea . . . the Coral Sea" might have been my last Bargello project—it was made in a flurry of redecorating prior to our daughter's wedding in 1991—but in May of 1992, I attended Alison Goss' "Designing to Music" workshop at the North Carolina Quilt Symposium. I signed up for that stimulating class without realizing that it would be Bargello one more time. In order to stretch myself, I decided to ignore the usual boundaries of Bargello. I eventually finished the "Fractured Rhapsody" begun that day and have explored related design ideas ever since.

In 1993, I began to teach at our local quilt shop, Sara Ballentine's Heirlooms and Comforts. In preparing notes for the classes, I ended up doing some computer renditions of new designs. My students kept asking, "Why don't you expand these notes and write a book?" Sara was a great help to me in organizing my material and in presenting my ideas before the quilting public.

Thanks to all of these friends, to my fellow Lake and Mountain Quilters who are so supportive of all the very creative members of our Guild, and to my new friends at That Patchwork Place—especially my technical editor, Laura Reinstatler, for her kindness and invaluable assistance. And thanks to my students who have shown me that we have just scratched the surface of possibilities in the Bargello world. I hope you have as much fun with this book as I have had in preparing it for you.

Dedication

I have the ingredient necessary for contented quilting—a husband who supports my habit and closes his eyes to the cotton/poly dust bunnies periodically drifting around. Dan even includes extra time on out-of-town trips so that I can stop in fabric shops along the way. He grew up in the quilting tradition; his mother made us a beautiful quilt for a wedding present that we will always treasure. I also have great parents who, like Dan, appreciated the results of all my various creative outbursts over the years and always encouraged me to try new ideas. And thanks to our children, who often found fabric on the kitchen table when it was long past time to find supper there instead. Without all of you, none of this would have been possible.

Marge Edie

Table of Contents

Introduction

Color, texture, and the feel of fabric on the bolt draw those of us who love the art of quilting into our favorite fabric shops. So many quilts . . . so many fabrics . . . so little time. Maybe these are the reasons that I love the Bargello techniques and the fast Quilt-As-You-Build-It construction; they combine speed, beauty, and technical achievement in fascinating ways.

Bargello has long been known as a type of needlepoint embroidery in which stitches are worked parallel to the grain of the fabric. Stitches are straight and are worked up or down from the previous stitch, creating a pattern. Flame patterns are especially popular. Bargello quilting techniques imitate this needlework tradition.

This book is designed to encourage you to experiment with color, texture, and contrast. Now may be the time to unorganize your storage shelves. Carefully grouping your fabric by color may actually inhibit the possibilities of some exciting combinations in your quilts. Bargello helps us go beyond our usual selection habits.

You will learn new designing and sewing skills to use in developing other quilt patterns. And, certainly, the fast Quilt-As-You-Build-It construction method lends itself to "Sunshine and Shadows," "Around the World," "Irish Chain," and many other traditional quilt designs.

First, you will learn how to do each step in "Basic Bargello Instruction," beginning on page 10, then examine the Bargello varieties in "Advanced Techniques" on pages 25-36. These steps prepare you to make the projects in the last section of the book. (See "The Patterns" on pages 45-88.) But beyond that, I hope you find creative stimulation from what you read in this book to use in future quilting endeavors. The possibilities are endless. I will just point you in the right direction so you can discover the rest of them for yourself.

Photo by Roy Ridge

Meet the Author

Marge Edie lives in Clemson, South Carolina, and is married to a professor of chemical engineering. She and Dan met at Ohio University, where Marge earned a bachelor of fine arts degree. She taught art in the Sandusky, Ohio, public schools, did a variety of free-lance design work and commissioned painting, and worked as a graphic artist in a printing company. After taking undergraduate and graduate courses in computer science, she worked for twelve years in the administrative programming services for Clemson University, developing computer systems for various offices on campus. Quilting crept up on her during this period. Several of Marge's quilts have been selected for the Hoffman Challenge traveling exhibits, and she has won numerous awards for her work. More recently, she has been teaching Bargello classes at Sara Ballentine's quilt shop, Heirlooms and Comforts, in Clemson, developing the ideas and techniques she presents in this book.

Definitions

A few terms that you may not be familiar with are used when making Bargello quilts. Take the time to familiarize yourself with the vocabulary to help master the techniques more quickly.

Bargello Strips: Strips of pieced fabric rectangles, created when strips are cut from color runs or when loops cut from the tube are opened.

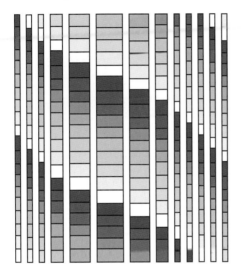

Bargello strips
(or Design Strips)

Blocks: Segments of a graphed curve that represent Bargello strip widths.

Color Run: A rectangle created by sewing several strips of fabric together.

Color-Run Strips: Strips of fabric sewn together into color runs.

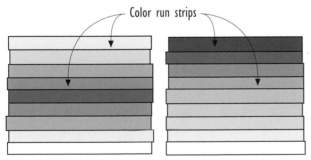

Color run strips

Two different color runs

Design Strips: See *Bargello Strips.*

Graphed Curve: A Bargello-design chart, indicating the design width, the size of the Bargello strips needed, how many to cut, and whether they will move up or down. The graph does not indicate the width of the color-run strips.

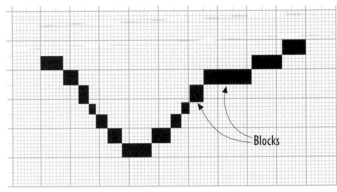

Blocks

Graphed curve

Loops: Strips cut from the tube, then opened up to form Bargello strips.

Tube: Two or more color runs sewn together to form a continuous tube of fabric.

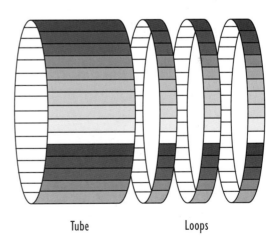

Tube   Loops

Tube Strips: See *Color-Run Strips.*

5

Tools and Fabric

Tools

You will need a rotary cutter, cutting mat, a 6" x 24" clear acrylic ruler and a 6" or 8" square acrylic ruler. Using these tools will become second nature to you after you complete your first Bargello quilt, if they are not already. A large (24" x 36") gridded cutting mat is best for these projects.

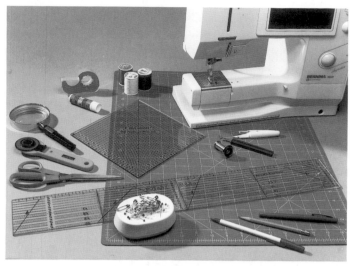

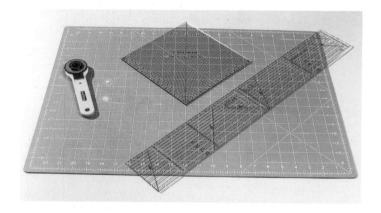

Use a properly working sewing machine with reliable tension control. The presser foot must not push down too hard onto the fabric or it will push the top layer of fabric forward faster than the bottom fabric.

You will probably need a seam ripper at some point—for straight lines that go curvy, for example. To make ripping out stitches easier, set the stitch length on your machine to ten stitches per inch and relax the thread tension just enough so that ripping out an error is possible.

Use long, round-headed pins. The standard, old-fashioned stainless steel pin with matching head is too hard on the fingers for all the pinning required.

You will need fabric shears, thread-snipping scissors, safety pins, thread to generally match the fabrics in your color run, and bobbin thread to match the backing.

When you are ready to design your own Bargello quilt, you may photocopy the graph paper in this book or purchase your own. To draw your own graphed curve, you will need a No. 2 pencil, an eraser, and transparent tape. Use a ball-point pen or felt-tip marker to check off the blocks along the graph as you complete them.

Fabric Selection: Color and Contrast Choices

For best results, choose the fabrics carefully. You do not need a full range from dark to light, bright to dull, complex to simple, but you should keep in mind several important considerations when selecting fabrics.

For the most exciting look in your finished product, select nine to fifteen different fabrics. For color ideas, find a color "indicator," such as a favorite painting or photograph. For "Explosion in Spring" on page 38, Betsy Hegg chose fabrics to match a floral oil painting done by her mother. The quilt hangs near it. "To the Sea . . . the Coral Sea" on page 40 was also designed to coordinate with colors found in artwork hanging nearby, so that the items are "tied together" by the Bargello quilt.

Another method quilters favor for design inspiration starts with one favorite fabric print. Select others to coordinate with the starting piece. Avoid choosing fabrics that are too related in color and texture—the final project will not have enough movement and spark. Keep in mind that a maverick color, print, or value (light or dark version of a color) may be just the accent your selection needs.

Remember to include a variety of textures in your final grouping. These add sparkle and zest to the curve. They also mask any tiny flaws and errors that may occur in your work. Solid fabrics are less desirable because they show every variance from perfectly straight seams.

Check out the wild combination in "Fractured Rhapsody" on page 84 to see what a charge the brilliant magenta and dull olive green give to the rich purples and golds. I chose magenta and dull olive green because, while they were not precisely included, I could "see" the colors in the other fabric prints. I started with the old gold, purple, and orange floral fabric (seen in the upper background fields), and I relied on inspiration when choosing the other fabrics. I wanted to suggest a feeling of loyalty and passion to match the musical mood in George Enesco's "Rumanian Rhapsody" during a workshop with Alison Goss.

After you have selected the fabrics, experiment with sequence. Arrange them from dark to light for maximum effect in a curve. Follow the order of the spectrum (rainbow), work from grayed to intense hues, or mix them up in a way that suits your own tastes. See the various ways illustrated below.

Fabric arranged from dark to light.

Fabrics arranged "out from the center," or value moving from one value at the center to its opposite value at each end.

After arranging your colors, record the sequence on paper with crayon or colored pencil, or glue a tiny trimming from each fabric on a color "map" for reference.

Computing Fabric Requirements

To calculate the amount of fabric required for a Bargello project, decide upon your quilt's finished size, then consider the number of different fabrics you have chosen for your color runs and the number of repeats of the color run you plan to use. Calculate how wide the strips of fabric should be cut (allowing $1/2$" for seam allowances) to cover the length of the quilt. For example, for a quilt 58" x 72", using 9 different fabrics in 3 color-run sequences, you will need 27 strips of fabric. The color run must equal 72" long when sewn together for a quilt without borders.

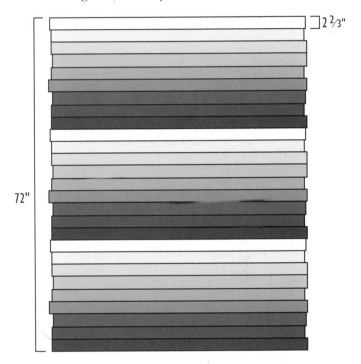

72" (length) ÷ 27 (total strips) = $2^2/3$"-wide strips (finished)

By changing the finished strip width to $2^1/2$", the color run's length shrinks to $67^1/2$", allowing room for top and bottom borders.

27 (total strips) x $2^1/2$" (strip width) = $67^1/2$" total length (leaving $4^1/2$" total for borders)

For wider borders, choose an even narrower color-run strip width:

27 x 2³/₈" = 64¹/₂" (leaving 7¹/₂" total or 3³/₄" for each top and bottom border)

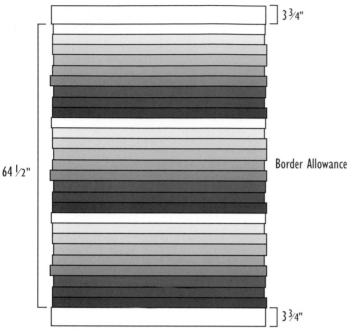

3³/₄"

64¹/₂"

Border Allowance

3³/₄"

Remember to add ¹/₂" for seam allowances to the strips. So, for 2³/₈"-wide finished strips, cut them 2⁷/₈" wide. This width includes enough for two ¹/₄"-wide seam allowances.

From the illustrations in this book, you can see that the drama of the Bargello curve is related to its steep slopes and contrasting gentle curves. If your color-run strips are too narrow, you will lose some of the steepness in your curve design. In other words, the wider the color-run strips, the more abrupt the curve design. (You can also control the pitch of the curves by how you move the Bargello strips up and down.) If you want to include narrow fabric strips in your color runs and tubes, you must cut narrow Bargello strips from the tubes to achieve the more dramatic slopes.

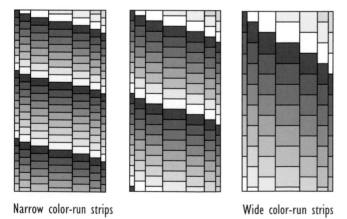

Narrow color-run strips   Wide color-run strips
Fewer color strips make steeper curves.

From each tube, you can cut Bargello strips to cover approximately 27" of Bargello width, depending upon the width and number of loops cut. For the 58"-wide quilt in this example, subtract 7¹/₂" for side borders to leave 50¹/₂" for the Bargello curve design. Make two tubes to cover the width of this quilt.

Finished Bargello section size

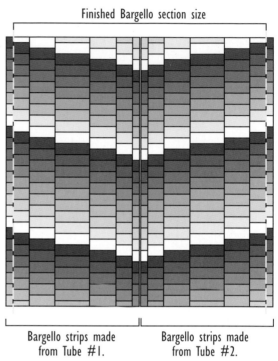

Bargello strips made   Bargello strips made
from Tube #1.   from Tube #2.

To figure the amount of yardage for each color, multiply the number of strips needed (6 strips, 3 for each tube) by the strip width (2⁷/₈"). Divide the total (17¹/₄") by 36" for the yardage requirement (0.479 yd. or ¹/₂ yd.).

6 x 2⁷/₈" = 17¹/₄" ÷ 36" = about ¹/₂ yard of each of the 9 colors

These amounts allow only a little bit extra for errors and trimming. To allow for cutting errors, plan to buy enough fabric to make another tube (perhaps a short one) if necessary. To allow for shrinkage, trimming dangling threads after laundering, and the possibility of constructing an extra, short tube, purchase an additional ¹/₂ to ⁵/₈ yard of each color.

¹/₂ yd. + ¹/₂ to ⁵/₈ yd. = 1 to 1¹/₈ yds. total of each of the 9 colors

Buy additional fabric if you would like to use the same fabric for borders, binding, or backing.

If you do need a bit more tubing, make a short one. Use one strip of each fabric, sew these into one color run, cut the run into three equal pieces, and sew these segments into one narrow tube. This smaller version will, after trimming, construct about 8" of Bargello design.

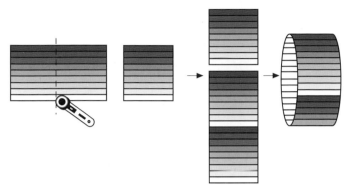

The number of tubes needed to construct the full width of a Bargello design also depends upon the number of Bargello strips required for the curves of your design. Too many steep slopes and, therefore, too many narrow Bargello strips use up the tubes more quickly than wide blocks in a design, because there will be more seams in the quilt. And of course, the more seams, the more work you will do. Try to keep a variety of Bargello strip widths in your design and let them average about one Bargello strip for each 1" of design width.

Use the examples on pages 7–8 to figure out the yardage requirements for any Bargello project. The following equation fits all traditional Bargello projects made from a tube:

$$\text{Amount of each fabric to purchase} = \left(\frac{\text{Length of finished Bargello}}{\text{Total number of strips in each tube}} + \frac{1}{2}"\right) \times \text{No. of strips of that color in a tube} \times \text{No. of Tubes (Bargello design width} \div 27") + \text{Any desired extra fabric for borders, backing, and errors}$$

TO RECAP:

1. Divide the finished Bargello length by the number of color-run strips your plan requires to get the finished strip width.

2. Add $\frac{1}{2}"$ for the seam allowances to that measurement. Cut the fabric strips this width.

3. Multiply the width from step 2 by the number of times that color strip is used in the Bargello length (the number of times it must be sewn into one of your tubes).

4. Multiply this by the number of tubes you will need. (One tube creates about 27" of finished Bargello width.) To find the number of tubes you need, divide the finished Bargello design width (total finished) by 27".

5. Add $\frac{1}{2}$–$\frac{5}{8}$ yd. extra for shrinkage and "error factor."

6. Add extra yardage for border and backing fabrics.

Basic Bargello Instruction

This section of the book covers all the steps a quilter must know to create a Quilt-As-You-Build-It Bargello piece. The steps interrelate in many ways, and it is important to understand each step and its relationship with the following steps. So read this over carefully, then scan it again to tie the steps together.

Once you understand the procedures, turn to the pattern section, beginning on page 45, and practice by making some quick Bargello place mats. These will prepare you for larger, traditional projects and also for the more complex ideas presented in the "Advanced Techniques" section on pages 25–36.

Preparing the Fabric

1. Wash and iron your fabric. Check for colorfastness; if the fabric bleeds when rinsed, continue rinsing until the water remains clear.

2. Fold fabric lengthwise, matching selvages, wrong sides together.

Fold

Selvages

3. Fold again, matching the first fold line to the selvage edges, creating four thicknesses.

4. For long yardage, accordion pleat each folded length of fabric into a pile that is about 6" x 10½". The fabric will pull easily across the cutting board as you cut strips and will be prefolded when set aside until it is needed later.

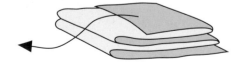

Cutting and Stitching Strips

1. Cut uneven edges off one end of the folded fabric before cutting strips. Align the folded fabric edge with the cutting mat's horizontal lines and align the ruler's lines along the vertical lines. Pressing down firmly on the ruler with your left hand; cut off the ragged edges, pushing the rotary cutter away from you. Reverse this procedure if you are left-handed.

N O T E

Some people line up the ruler on the other side of the fabric to cut strips. Practice with scrap fabrics to see which method you prefer.

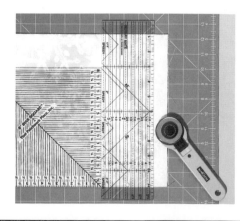

2. To cut strips, place the fabric to the right and measure from the left cut edges. Cut, making sure to cut through all fabric layers.

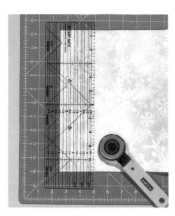

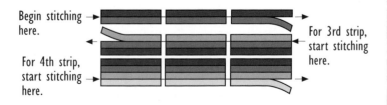

✦

N O T E

The width of the color run will be the width of the narrowest fabric you use—40" to 45" wide from selvage to selvage. (Fabric widths vary with manufacturers and shrinkage after laundering.)

TIP: Do not cut all the fabric strips to the shortest strip's length. Trim later, after all the strips have been sewn into the tube. If you use one fabric that is much narrower than the other fabrics, cut two or more strips, then piece them together end to end before sewing the pieced strip into the color run. A seam in one of your color-run strips will not be noticeable.

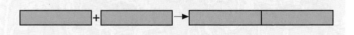

3. Sew the cut strips together into color runs by chain piecing. To chain piece, stitch a continuous seam without lifting the presser foot or cutting the threads between strips. After you have completed stitching all the strips of one fabric, clip the threads between units. Turn the color run around and sew a new strip at the end of the strip, where you just finished stitching.

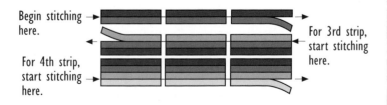

Begin stitching here.
For 3rd strip, start stitching here.
For 4th strip, start stitching here.

This is important to prevent stretching the strips unevenly as you sew. When successive newly added strips

stretch, the color run bows, making it more difficult to cut accurate perpendicular Bargello strips.

TIP: With each strip, place a pin at the end of the stitching line so you will know which end to begin stitching when adding the next strip.

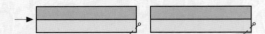

TIP: If you keep even-numbered fabric strips on top when stitching and odd-numbered strips on the bottom, you will automatically begin stitching each new strip to opposite ends of the color run.

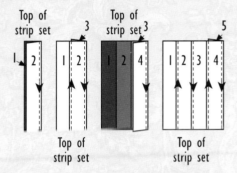

Top of strip set
Top of strip set
Top of strip set
Top of strip set

TIP: As you add each new strip, look back to the shortest strip in the run. Roughly align the ends of the new strip with the ends of the shortest strip, placing the new strip so that there will be no excess waste at either end. In diagram A below, the bottom strip of the color run has been aligned too far to the right, creating waste at one end. In diagram B below, the bottom strip has been aligned with the shortest strip in the color run, making better use of the length.

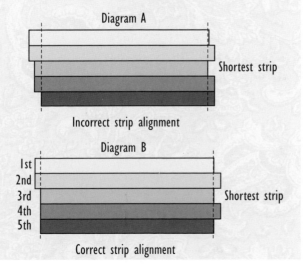

Diagram A

Shortest strip

Incorrect strip alignment

Diagram B

1st
2nd
3rd
4th
5th

Shortest strip

Correct strip alignment

4. When constructing the color run, make sure to align the strips into a rectangular unit instead of a parallelogram so the tube doesn't twist when it is sewn together.

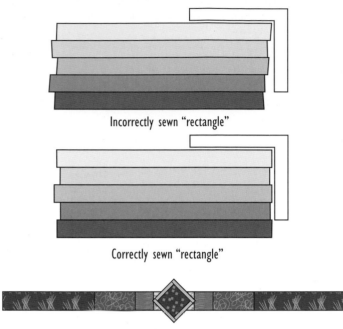

Incorrectly sewn "rectangle"

Correctly sewn "rectangle"

Constructing Tubes

1. Sew one or more color runs into a continuous tube. Your project's size and design will determine how many color runs you sew into the tube.

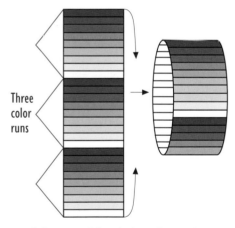

Three color runs

Be careful to avoid twisting the color run when sewing it into a tube, or the Bargello strips you cut from it will contain parallelograms rather than rectangles.

This is not fatal (and will occur a little bit, no matter how careful you are) but should be minimized as much as possible.

2. After completing the tubes, press the seam allowances in the same direction unless you are planning a matched-seam construction. (See "Matched Seams" on page 16.)

3. Fold the tube in half or in thirds lengthwise, creating four to six thicknesses of fabric. Make sure the folded lengths are even and smooth, and accordion-pleat them if necessary.

4. Trim off the uneven selvages by carefully lining up the folds with the lines on the cutting mat and cutting perpendicular to the folds. Make sure to trim off the uneven edges through all four or six thicknesses before you begin cutting your first strip.

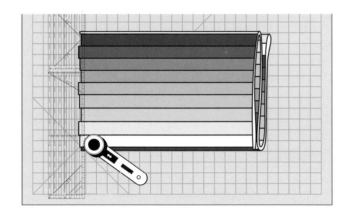

5. Cut loops from the tube. Refer to your graphed design for the width of the loops. (See "Designing a Curve" on pages 13-14.) Remember to add ½" for seam allowances.

> **TIP:** Occasionally, even Bargello strips cut from a correctly sewn tube become angled. Take some time to realign the tube on the gridded cutting mat, cutting a wedge if necessary to square up the end of the tube, then continue cutting perpendicular strips.
>
>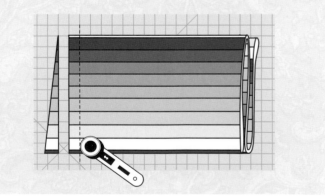

Now the tedious work is over and will soon pay off with a beautiful project!

Designing a Curve

One key to a great Bargello quilt is designing a great curve. With a little practice, you can design a continuous curve and translate it into blocks that represent the width of the loops you cut from the tube.

1. Choose graph paper with small squares (e.g., ten per inch). Each square will represent 1/4".

2. Disregard the vertical dimensions of each square. These correspond to the width of the color-run strips you cut for the tube construction and vary from project to project.

3. On graph paper, draw the width of the Bargello project you want to create and sketch a graceful curved line across the width of the Bargello design area.

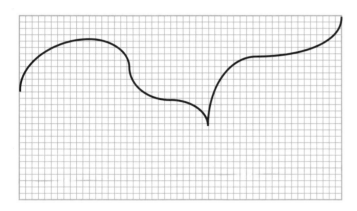

4. Determine the size of each block required to imitate the direction your curve is taking. Fill in graph squares to represent the width of Bargello strips needed for your design.

    A. Create steep slopes with narrow vertical blocks.
    B. Create gradual slopes from wide vertical blocks.
    C. Create points with graduated narrow blocks that change direction.
    D. Create waves with graduated wide blocks that change direction.

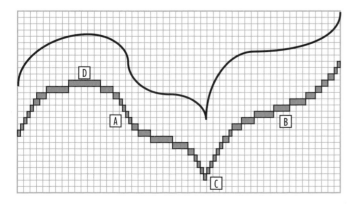

Mastering this last set of steps requires a bit of practice, but after the first few blocks, the process becomes more comfortable. Start with a pencil so you can erase, and use some of the examples shown in the book. The measurements of your blocks should change gradually as your curve changes; to ensure graceful lines, avoid large "jumps" in block widths. Even if your curve includes dynamic, jutting slopes, plan the block widths so these slopes are graceful. Make use of repetitions in block width to achieve the slope length and curve size that you drew.

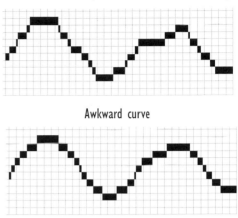

Awkward curve

Graceful curve

Remember that each square across on the graph paper represents 1/4" of the finished fabric strip. Add 1/2" to each block for seam allowances when you cut a loop from your tube. A good rule of thumb is to include approximately the same number of blocks as the number of inches in the width. For example, for a 40"-wide design, include about 40 blocks, and therefore strips, in varying widths.

For sparkling colors and exciting designs, plan your curve to include an interesting balance between wide and narrow blocks. Remember, many narrow blocks in the design mean more seams, so the quilt will be heavier than if it includes many wide strips. Bargello strips wider than about 3" will not be held down as firmly as narrower ones, but these can be quilted later to hold them down more securely.

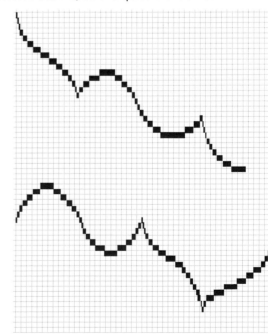

Two different design curves

You will refer to your graph-paper pattern as you progress across your quilt, so make it easy to read. Darken the blocks with a ball-point pen when you are satisfied with the design. As you cut loops from the tube and sew them into place, mark off each one on the graph paper so that you don't accidentally skip or repeat design segments. Check off finished parts of your graph neatly so that you can use it again if you wish. I have reused charted designs for more than one project.

Once you have graphed a pleasing pattern, the quilt is well on its way, and the most complicated steps are behind you.

Preparing the Backing and Batting

For best results, choose a lightweight batting with even thickness and minimal loft. I prefer flannel with a pale lengthwise stripe, as long as it doesn't show through the lightest-color fabric. Needlepunch, a thin white fleece sold off the bolt in discount or fabric stores, works well, as does flannel printed with a 2" grid to help you keep strips aligned.

1. Wash and iron the backing fabric, then construct the backing to your size requirements. Make it about 4" larger on all sides than the desired size of your finished project, including borders and binding. If you are using flannel as batting, wash and iron it and piece it as necessary to match the backing.

Make the seam for the batting as inconspicuous as possible. Overlap the raw edges of the batting and stitch, zigzagging on top as shown.

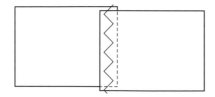

2. Place the backing wrong side up and lay the batting on top. Working from the center to the sides, smooth out the wrinkles. If you use a striped or gridded flannel, place it upside down on the backing so that the stripe shows through to the front as little as possible.

3. Secure the two layers with safety pins placed in a grid pattern every 8" across the entire surface. Remove the pins as you attach the Bargello strips.

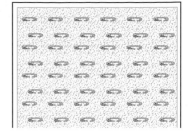

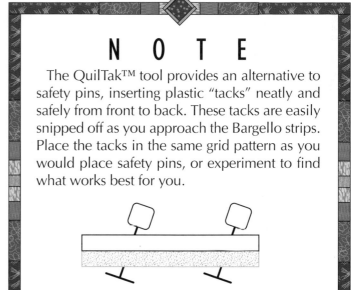

N O T E

The QuilTak™ tool provides an alternative to safety pins, inserting plastic "tacks" neatly and safely from front to back. These tacks are easily snipped off as you approach the Bargello strips. Place the tacks in the same grid pattern as you would place safety pins, or experiment to find what works best for you.

4. With a pencil, draw a line along the exact middle of the batting from top to bottom. Make sure the line is straight and perpendicular to the top and bottom since it is the guide for the first Bargello strip. Align subsequent Bargello strips by referring to the first strip.

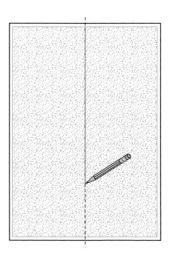

5. Mark one horizontal line across the center from side to side. Refer to this line to match the center of the Bargello strips as you pin them down.

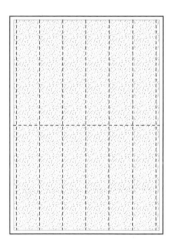

TIP: To avoid excess weight and bulk while constructing a king- or queen-size spread, make the quilt in three vertical sections. First, cut and prepare only the center section's backing and batting, then sew on the Bargello strips. Sew the strips all the way to each edge of the center section.

Prepare one outer section of backing and batting. Place the center section's backing on top of the outer section's backing, right sides together, and pin the next Bargello strip along the edge of the center section, right sides together. Stitch through all layers at once, adding both the new Bargello strip and outer section. Press lightly, if necessary, and continue adding Bargello strips until you reach the outside edge. If the side of the center section occurs at a point where you can't use the same stitching line for adding a strip, stitch the batting and backing together, then continue adding strips.

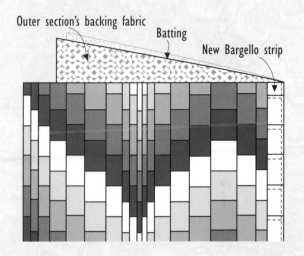

Repeat with the second outer section on the remaining side.

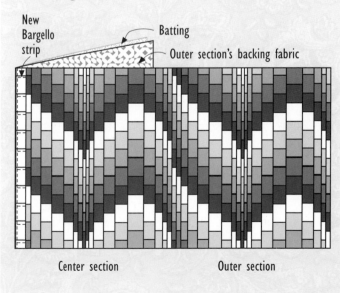

Sewing the Bargello Strips

Now the fun begins!

1. After trimming off the selvage edges from the tube strips, carefully check through the layers to make sure that the edges are even with no rough spots.

2. Determine whether your design will include staggered seams or matched seams. Matched seams run in horizontal lines across the quilt from one side to the other. In staggered seam construction, the horizontal seam lines are staggered and do not meet as the strips cross the quilt. Seams will be staggered automatically if the color-run strips are cut to different widths, although strips cut to the same widths may be staggered also, depending upon the curve.

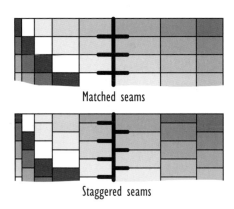

Matched seams

Staggered seams

Matched Seams: As you cut each loop from the tube, pull out stitches between two fabric rectangles and match the Bargello strip ends in a straight line across the top of the quilt.

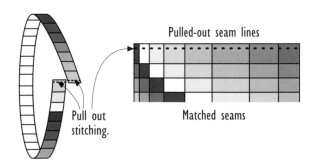

Pulled-out seam lines

Pull out stitching.

Matched seams

TIP: The seam intersections create some bulk unless you do a little trick: iron one tube's seam allowances clockwise and the other's seam allowances counterclockwise, then alternate tubes when cutting Bargello strips that will be sewn next to each other. If the seam allowances in adjoining Bargello strips lie in opposite directions, they will match up easily if you butt seams against each other before stitching.

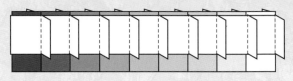

Staggered Seams: As you cut loops from the tube, pull out the threads in one seam in the first loop to create a Bargello strip. Cut through the center of the rectangle of desired fabric in the next loop for the next Bargello strip. Continue by alternately pulling threads and cutting strips.

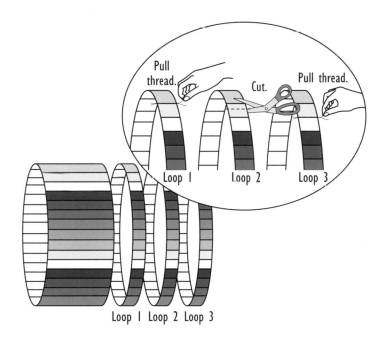

Pull thread.　　Cut.　　Pull thread.

Loop 1　　Loop 2　　Loop 3

Loop 1　Loop 2　Loop 3

Sew the strips to the quilt, matching the edge of each cut Bargello strip with the pulled-out seam line of the adjacent strip as shown, creating an uneven edge across the top of the quilt.

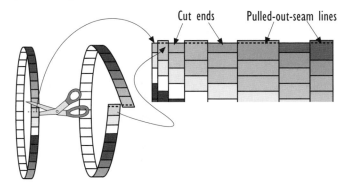

Cut ends   Pulled-out-seam lines

3. Referring to steps 4 and 5 of "Constructing Tubes" on page 12 and your graphed curve for the width of the center strip, cut the first Bargello loop from the tube, making sure to add 1/2" for seam allowances. (In the example below, the center block spans three 1/4" squares representing a finished measurement of 3/4" and must be cut 1 1/4".) After cutting, make sure you have cut through all thicknesses of the tube before lifting the ruler.

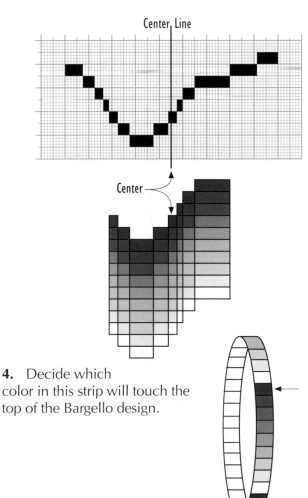

Center Line

Center

4. Decide which color in this strip will touch the top of the Bargello design.

5. Remove the stitches in the seam at the top of that color in the loop to make a Bargello strip.

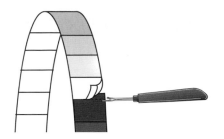

6. Gently stretch out the strip, right sides up, along the central (*vertical*) pencil line. This first strip may not be centered precisely over the center line (depending on its location on the graphed curve), so refer to your graphed curve for proper placement to one side or the other.

The middle of the Bargello strip will cross the *horizontal* pencil line either at a seam line or a fabric rectangle. Match the seam line or find and crease the center of the rectangle crosswise and match that fold mark to the horizontal pencil line on the batting.

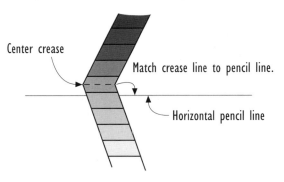

Center crease

Match crease line to pencil line.

Horizontal pencil line

7. With the Bargello strip in place, pin securely to the backing in each fabric rectangle.

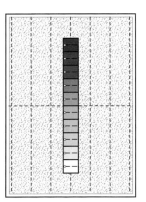

8. Refer to the graphed curve for the dimensions of the Bargello strip to the right of the center strip. From these dimensions, cut the next loop from the tube, remembering to add 1/2" for seam allowances. Note whether the strip moves up or down the curve. If it moves up the curve, find the rectangle of fabric that matches the one at the *top* of the center Bargello strip. Cut in half across this rectangle to open the loop.

If the second strip moves down the curve, find the rectangle of fabric that matches the one at the *bottom* of the center Bargello strip. Cut in half across this rectangle to open the loop.

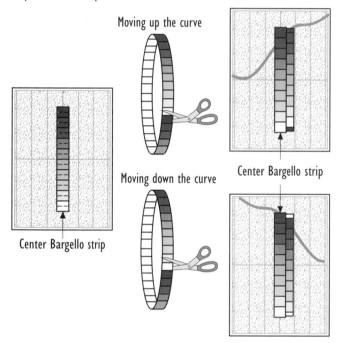

Moving up the curve

Moving down the curve

Center Bargello strip

Center Bargello strip

9. Match the middle of this Bargello strip to the horizontal pencil line and to the center point of the previously sewn Bargello strip. Line up each cut end of this Bargello strip with the pulled-out seam lines at each end of the previous strip. The top and bottom of the Bargello strips are offset vertically by 1/4". (See the illustration for "Staggered Seams" on page 16.)

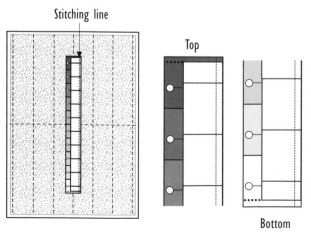

Stitching line

Top

Bottom

18 BASIC BARGELLO INSTRUCTION

TIP: Pinning the Bargello strip at every seam line helps when feeding the quilt through the machine. Place the pins parallel to the seam line when pinning, with the points pointing toward the sewing machine. This makes it easy to remove each pin as the strip feeds through the machine.

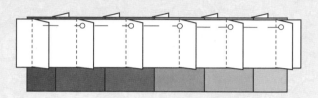

10. Pin the seam allowances so they face the same direction in which they were originally pressed and remove pins as they are about to reach the presser foot to keep the seams lined up. Pulling a pin out too early may distort the Bargello strip, so that the finished product will not be a rectangle.

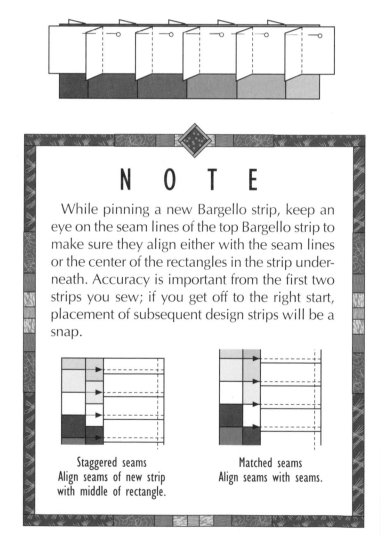

N O T E

While pinning a new Bargello strip, keep an eye on the seam lines of the top Bargello strip to make sure they align either with the seam lines or the center of the rectangles in the strip underneath. Accuracy is important from the first two strips you sew; if you get off to the right start, placement of subsequent design strips will be a snap.

Staggered seams
Align seams of new strip with middle of rectangle.

Matched seams
Align seams with seams.

11. Machine stitch the Bargello strips with straight seam lines. Use a seam ripper to carefully remove only the crooked part of any "glitch" that may occur.

12. For each seam, pull the bobbin threads to the front from the backing so they can be hidden by subsequent design strips. Knot the top threads if you wish and let the ends hang. They will be covered by borders and binding.

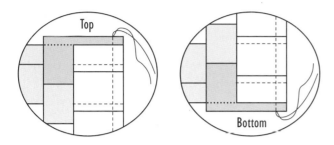

13. As you sew each Bargello strip onto the quilt, flip it over to the right or left, press if necessary, pin it smoothly and tightly, then pin down the next strip in the design sequence.

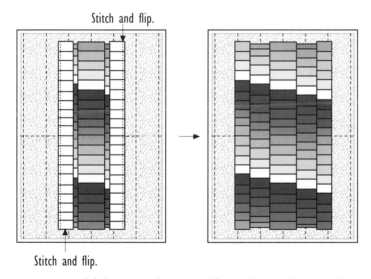

Stitch and flip.

Stitch and flip.

Be careful that you do not pull out the stitching in the rectangles before the strip is sewn into the quilt. If a little of this stitching comes undone, don't worry; it will be held firmly by the next design strip in the pattern as it is sewn to the backing.

TIP: Every time you flip a Bargello strip that comes close to one of the vertical pencil lines, check to make sure your stitching lines remain straight and parallel with these lines. If a seam line wavers, adjust the next stitching line when sewing down the next Bargello strip. Narrow or widen the seam just a bit so that, when you flip the next Bargello strip, it will be a little straighter or more parallel. Make adjustments on the wider Bargello strips only; the variation in seam and strip width will not be noticeable. It may take several strips before the strips and lines are parallel again.

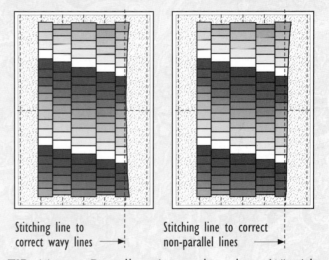

Stitching line to correct wavy lines ⟶

Stitching line to correct non-parallel lines ⟶

TIP: Narrow Bargello strips, such as those ¼" wide, are nice to include in a design for dramatic, steep slopes and bold points. I like to include three or four of these strips together in a few parts of my curve.

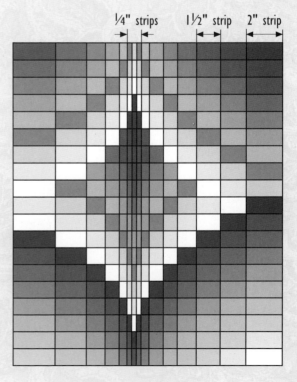

¼" strips   1½" strip   2" strip

TIP: Stitching ¼"-wide (finished) design strips to a uniform width is difficult, posing a challenge if sewn in the typical manner. Sew these strips more easily by inserting the pins in the opposite direction from usual.

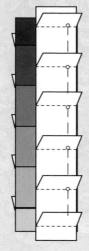

Turn the quilt around, with the top of the quilt at the bottom. Pin the new strip to the quilt (the pins will automatically be positioned to pull out easily).

Flip the quilt over and sew the seam from the backing side, lining up your presser foot with the previous seam line. Reach under the quilt to pull out pins from the front as you stitch, checking to see that your seam allowances are flat. Remember to reverse the thread colors in the machine so the stitching matches the other seams on the back.

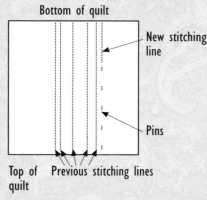

TIP: When stitching Bargello strips to the backing, watch carefully when placing strips to make sure the ends extend in a straight line across the top and bottom of the quilt. Avoid stretching the strips unevenly when adding them to the backing. When the quilt is completed, the sewn strips should form a rectangle, not an hourglass or a parallelogram.

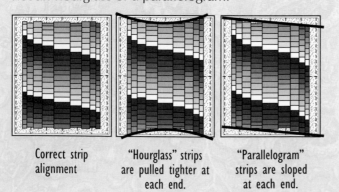

Correct strip alignment

"Hourglass" strips are pulled tighter at each end.

"Parallelogram" strips are sloped at each end.

TIP: Measure occasionally to see that the design width agrees with your originally graphed design. For example, after being stitched to the backing, Bargello strips that represent a total of thirty-three graph squares across the paper design should measure 8¼" of finished width. (Thirty-three graph squares, representing ¼" each, equals 8¼".) Consistent ¼"-wide seams will help achieve this. Seams sewn too narrowly cause the strips to reach the quilt's width before the design curve is finished. Seams sewn wider than ¼" narrow the strips, depleting the strip supply before the design is finished.

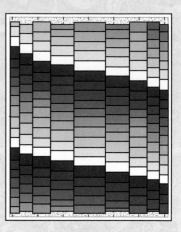

Seam allowances sewn narrower than ¼".

Seam allowances sewn wider than ¼".

You may need to make a change in your graphed design, either by adding or subtracting a Bargello strip from your original plan. A good time to do this is at the outer right and left edges, depending upon the curve.

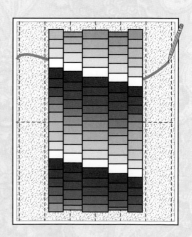

TIP: If you must take a break from your Bargello construction, insert about four pins near the cut end of the tube, securing the edges so they remain straight and aligned. When you return to your work, you won't have to waste tubing by retrimming rough edges.

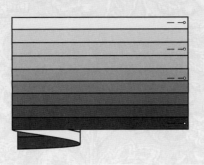

After learning these basics, it's just a matter of working your way to the edges of the graphed design and seeing the beautiful Bargello quilt come to life!

Borders

Most Bargello quilts look best with simple borders. However, when I constructed "To the Sea . . . the Coral Sea" on page 40, I wanted the finished queen-size spread to say "Quilt!" to anyone who saw it, so I designed a complex series of borders. The size of the design area warranted a dramatic finished edge.

In a smaller quilt, a complicated border may detract from the visual strength of the project. Experiment on paper to see what you like.

Attach border strips in the same way that you sew design strips onto the quilt: Stitch one strip at a time, then flip it over and press if necessary. Adding the borders in this manner gives a nice firm edge to the quilt. Stitch the side borders first, then the top and bottom borders.

1. Measure through the center of the quilt from raw edge to raw edge (top to bottom) when determining how long to cut your side borders. Cut the strips, joining if necessary, to match this measurement. Sewing the strips through the batting and backing tends to "eat up" the length of the strips a bit, so it may be necessary to add a little extra length.

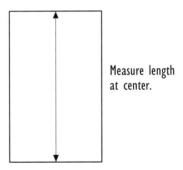

Measure length at center.

2. Referring to the diagram below, mark or place a pin at the center and quarter points along the outside edges of the quilt. Repeat with the border strips.

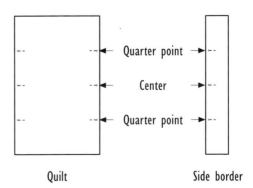

Quilt   Side border

3. Position the side border strips to hide small imperfections in the Bargello strips' straight edges. Pin the border to the quilt, matching ends and marked points, pinning along the edges, and easing fullness if necessary. Sew side borders to quilt.

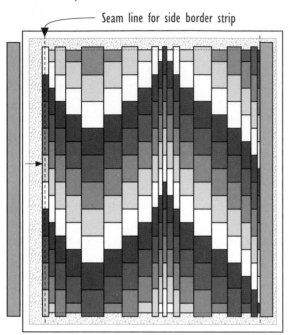

Seam line for side border strip

4. For the top and bottom borders, measure through the center of the quilt from raw edge to raw edge, including the side borders, and cut the strips to this measurement.

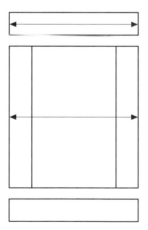

5. Align the raw edges of the top and bottom border strips with the cut end of the Bargello strips. The offset Bargello strips (with pulled-out seam allowances) extend $1/4$" beyond the border strips ($1/2$" beyond the seam line). Pin and sew the top and bottom borders to the quilt as you did for the side borders.

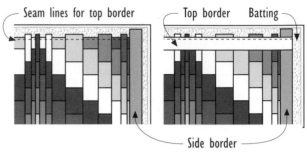

Seam lines for top border — Top border — Batting

Side border

Cornerstones may be added for contrast or to give additional emphasis to colors in the piece.

1. Measure and cut top, bottom, and side borders before adding them to the quilt. Attach side borders first.

2. Cut corner squares' dimensions equal to the cut width of the border strips. For example, if border strips are cut $3^1/2$" wide, cut $3^1/2$" x $3^1/2$" squares.

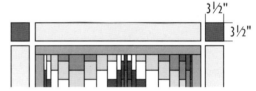

$3^1/2$"
$3^1/2$"

3. Stitch squares to each end of the top and bottom border strips, then sew borders to the quilt.

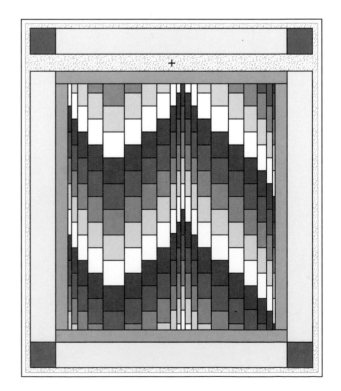

Binding

I generally "cheat" by not cutting binding on the bias and find the results satisfactory. Mitered corners in the binding are a must—their "polished points" correspond well with the precision of the Bargello design.

1. Decide how wide you want the binding to be. Trim the backing and batting to the outer measurements of the quilt. The distance from the outer border strip's stitching line to the outer edge will be the width of your binding. For example, if you want a $1\frac{1}{2}$" bound edge, trim the backing and batting so that $1\frac{1}{4}$" extends beyond the outer border. If you prefer a more traditional $\frac{1}{4}$"–$\frac{3}{8}$" binding, trim the backing and batting even with the raw edge of the outer border strip.

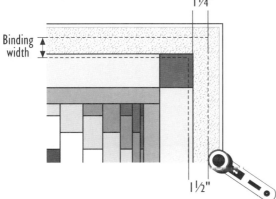

2. For single-thickness binding, cut the strips two times the finished width, plus $\frac{1}{2}$" for seams. For instance, if the bound edge is to be $1\frac{1}{2}$" wide, cut the binding strips $3\frac{1}{2}$" wide. Cut enough strips to go all the way around, including 6 strip widths' extra length for overlapped seams and corners.

For double-thickness binding, cut the strips four times the width of the edge, plus $\frac{1}{2}$" for seams ($6\frac{1}{2}$"-wide strips in this case).

3. Piece your binding strips with 45°-angle seams to reduce bulk.

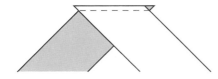

N O T E

For double-thickness binding, fold the strips in half lengthwise with right sides out and press. Match the binding's raw edges with the outer border's raw edges and stitch. Do not open the double-thickness binding when sewing it to the quilt. After stitching the binding to the quilt, fold the binding over and stitch to the back of the quilt along the binding's fold.

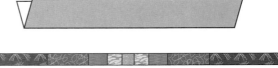

4. Place the binding strip along the raw edges of the border as shown. Leaving 3" free at the beginning of the binding, stitch, using a $\frac{1}{4}$"-wide seam. Stop stitching $\frac{1}{4}$" from the end of the border strip.

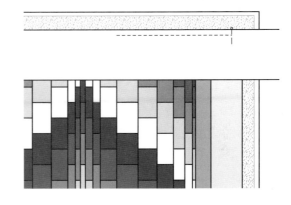

5. Fold the binding away from the quilt, creating a 45° fold as shown.

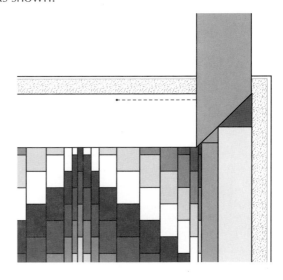

6. Fold the binding back at the *edge of the quilt* and align the binding's raw edges with the edges of the border strip. Starting at the outer edge of the quilt, stitch, using a ¼"-wide seam allowance.

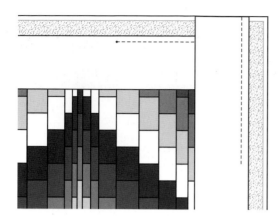

7. Stitch binding to all four sides and miter the corners as directed in steps 5 and 6. Lap the end of the binding over the beginning. The overlap should equal two times the width of the binding. Cut a 45° angle on each end as shown.

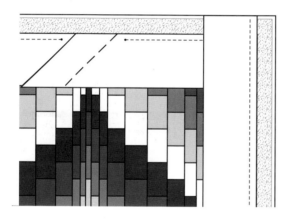

8. Trim the uncut end to overlap ½". With right sides together, stitch, using a ¼"-wide seam allowance.

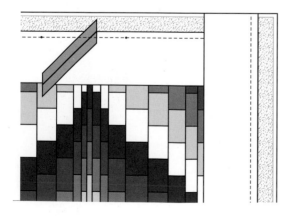

9. Turn the binding to the back and sew in place, using a blind hem stitch. For single-thickness binding, fold under ¼" on the raw edge and sew down neatly to the seam line on the back. For double-thickness binding, stitch along the folded edge.

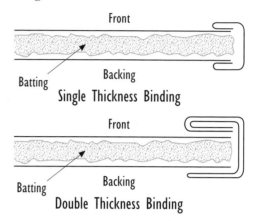

10. Miter corners on both sides as you stitch the binding to the back. If desired, stitch along the miter fold.

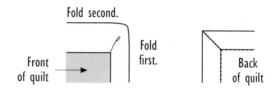

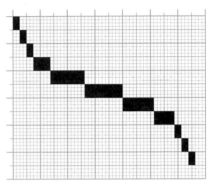

Advanced Techniques

If you feel comfortable turning a charted curve into a Bargello quilt, and you understand the "Quilt-As-You-Build-It" construction, you are ready to have a lot of fun with variations on the Bargello theme.

Read over the following suggestions for changing the basic Bargello curve structure. Use these ideas to stimulate your imagination, so you can alter and augment the Bargello designs.

Keeping the different color runs separate, rather than sewing them into a tube, allows for more Bargello strip combinations and manipulations. Many of the designs in this book were developed using color-run paper. Some of this paper can be found on pages 92-94. Cutting paper strips and experimenting with their placement prevents wasting fabric later.

Using one design curve, I will discuss some of the variations possible. Changes to this starting curve will be made as more complicated curve areas are needed to illustrate a point.

Some of the following suggestions are shown with matched seam construction and some with staggered seam construction. Either method of Bargello quilting applies to the advanced techniques suggested here.

Variations on the Theme

Start with a basic curve design.

Substitute straight lines of the same fabric in vertical and/or horizontal rectangles or strips. Before sewing the Bargello strips to the backing, remove rectangles from the strips, then add rectangles or strips of different fabric. Choose fabric that appears elsewhere in the color run, or use new fabric.

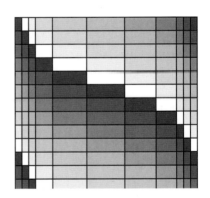

Graph for the basic design

1. To add horizontal lines of fabric, remove single rectangles or partial strips from the Bargello strips.

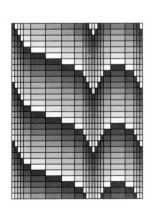

Basic curve

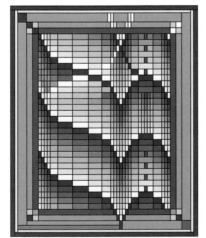

Curve with variations

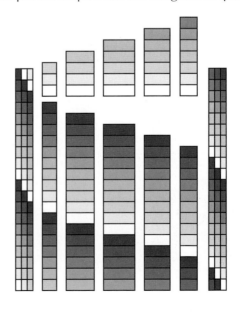

2. Sew single rectangles into strips, then add to the Bargello strip.

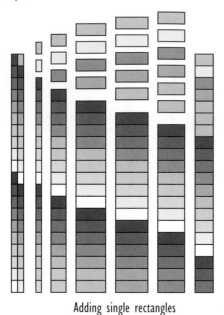

Adding single rectangles

OR Sew a partial color run, cut into strips to match the width of each corresponding Bargello strip, and add to the Bargello strips as shown below. Remove or add more rectangles from the partial color run strips as needed before adding to the Bargello strips.

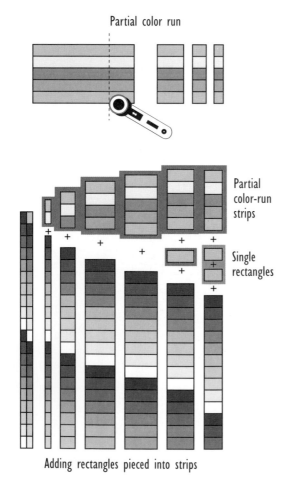

Partial color run

Partial color-run strips

Single rectangles

Adding rectangles pieced into strips

For examples of adding rectangles or strips of fabrics to the design, see "Fireflies" on pages 72-76 or "Fractured Rhapsody" on pages 84-88. In "Fractured Rhapsody," the upper dark section of the quilt is made of unseamed strips of one fabric, causing the Bargello design to appear to "float" in front of a background. For "Fireflies," rectangles of the same fabric sewn into Bargello strips make up the small dark sections at the top and bottom.

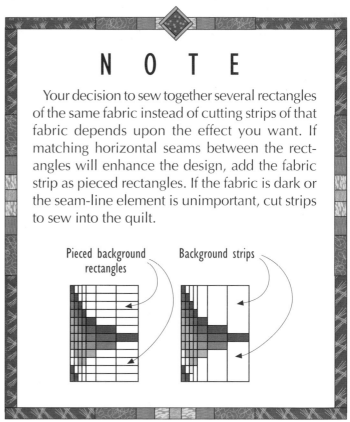

N O T E

Your decision to sew together several rectangles of the same fabric instead of cutting strips of that fabric depends upon the effect you want. If matching horizontal seams between the rectangles will enhance the design, add the fabric strip as pieced rectangles. If the fabric is dark or the seam-line element is unimportant, cut strips to sew into the quilt.

Pieced background rectangles

Background strips

3. To add vertical lines to the Bargello design, add rectangles or a strip of one fabric to the Bargello strip in vertical rows.

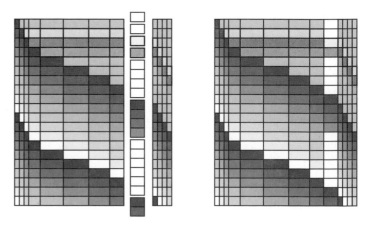

4. Manipulate the rectangles to "bend" the curve in another direction.

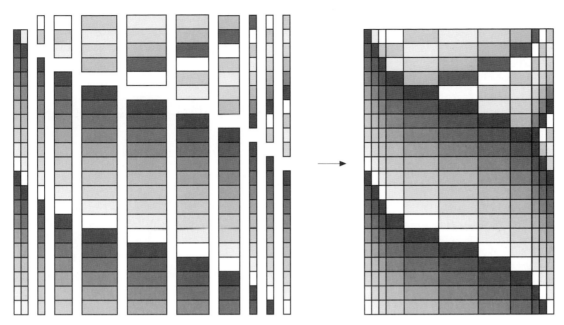

"Bending" the curve in a new direction.

5. To achieve a woven look, cut a wide Bargello strip, remove alternating rectangles, and cut the rectangles in half vertically. Insert rectangles of fabric as shown and resew to make the Bargello strip.

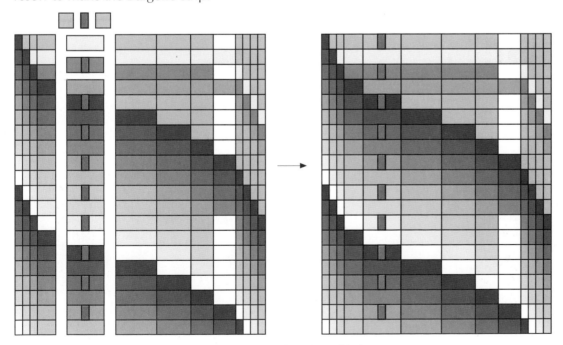

Inserting rectangles for a "woven" look.

6. Instead of inserting a plain fabric rectangle for the woven effect in step 5 above, set in or appliqué a piece of lace, ribbon, or metallic braid on top of the fabric rectangle, then sew into the Bargello strip.

Using Separator Strips

Separator strips are stitched into the quilt between Bargello strips. They are a challenge to keep totally parallel if you make them too narrow, but they can eliminate bulky seam crossings in matched seam constructions.

◆ Repeat a fabric from your color run or choose a new fabric.

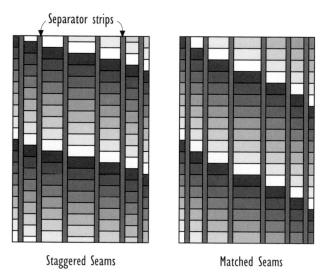

Separator strips

Staggered Seams   Matched Seams

◆ Choose Bargello strips from your color run but place them in different progressions from the Bargello strips in the primary design. Try creating a secondary curve with these additional strips. In the illustrations below and at right, notice how the separator strips and the Bargello strips become equally important when each set of strips is cut the same width.

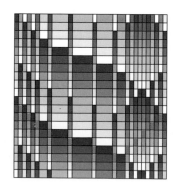
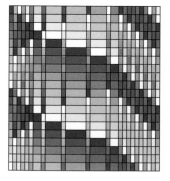

◆ Alternate two different color runs. Here, the rules disappear with regard to matching seam lines. Sew one color run from dark colors, the other one from light colors, constructing them with color-run strips of different widths. Repeat their sequence identically across the quilt or shift their position to create a secondary pattern. This is a good way to use leftover color runs from other projects.

Separator strips sewn in identical sequence.

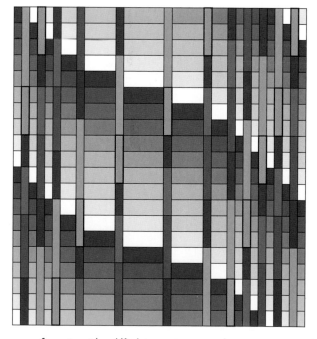

Separator strips shifted to create a secondary pattern.

Exploring Curves

◆ Add complementary curve lines. Two mirror-image curves that move in identical arcs but in opposite directions are called complementary curves. For example, if a curve moves from a point at the center of the left edge of the quilt to the upper right corner of the quilt, its complement would move from the same starting point to the lower right corner of the quilt. If one curve moves to the right 1" and up 1" on the graph, its complement would move to the right 1" and down 1".

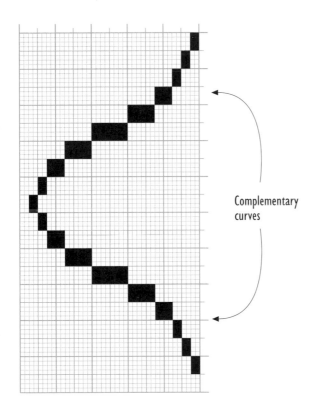

Complementary curves

If you use an *odd* number of fabrics in the color run, the point where two curves meet will contain two identical fabric rectangles. This could be a problem if the rectangles are large and distort the curve or if they distract from the Bargello design.

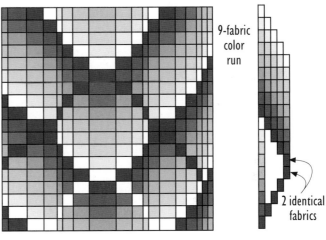

9-fabric color run

2 identical fabrics

Double blocks of one fabric appear where odd-numbered color runs connect.

Odd number of fabrics

With an even number of fabrics in the color run, any curve can rejoin another one without repeating two fabrics. Compare the curves in the illustrations above and below to see the difference.

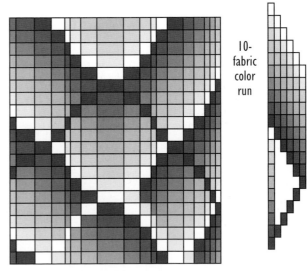

10-fabric color run

With an even-numbered color run, a single block of one fabric appears.

Even number of fabrics

◆ Opening Bargello strips, adding parts of Bargello strips "upside down," and removing rectangles from other Bargello strips in the design create "east-west" peaks and waves in the design.

In the diagrams below, the color-run order of most of the Bargello strips in the quilt is shown at left. At the left side of the quilt, Bargello strips A through E are placed end to end in this order. Moving to the right, the center section of Strip F includes two rectangles, 9 and 10, from the same color run, but the order is reversed or "upside down." Strip G's center section contains three rectangles (8, 9, and 10) in reverse order. Note that all the added strips are reversed, and a new rectangle is included at the lower end of the strip as the strips move across the quilt. Note also that rectangles are removed from the upper Bargello strips as the center strips are added.

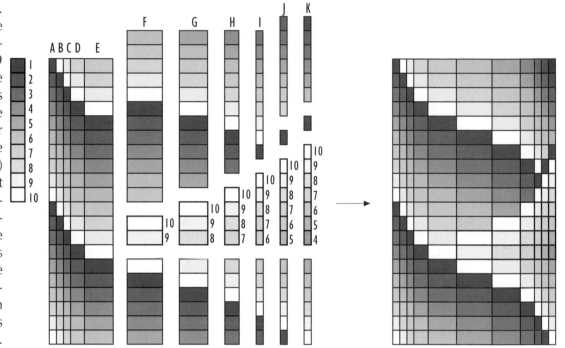

◆ Create a mirror image by cutting or separating loops at different rectangles, then reversing one strip as it is sewn to the end of another identical strip.

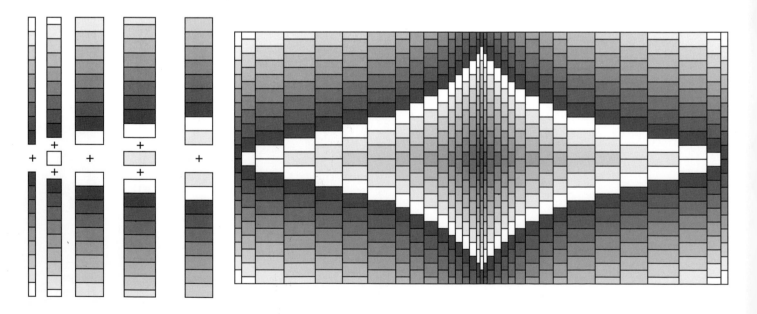

◆ Create large areas of background using one fabric. Cut a wide strip of this fabric to sew into the color run instead of cutting out and attaching individual rectangles in the Bargello strips. Because this reduces the number of seams, it helps keep the strips' measurements consistent when cutting loops from your tube.

◆ Create intricate areas, intensifying curve details with narrow color-run strip widths. This is done either by sewing narrow strips into the color run or by cutting them narrower and resewing them together after they are cut off the tube.

Consider making a second color run using the same order of fabrics, but this time cut each color-run strip narrower than those in the primary color run. In the diagram below, the center section of the design is made of color-run strips cut one-half the width of the primary color-run strips.

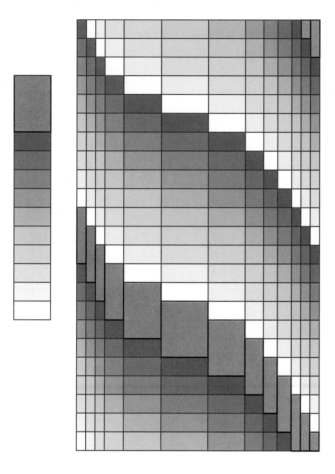

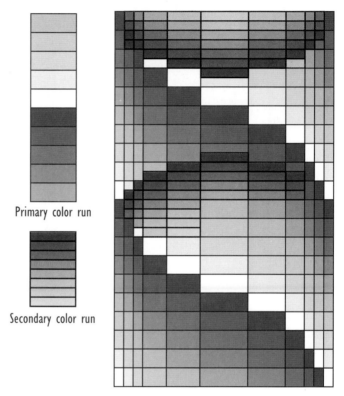

Primary color run

Secondary color run

Changes in horizontal strip width.

◆ Change the width of the rectangles in one area by removing one or more original rectangles in the color run and substituting several small rectangles. If the finished Bargello strip is 2¼" wide, for example, three finished rectangles, each ¾" wide, can be inserted into that space. For larger, more complex areas, cut narrow Bargello strips, stitch them together side by side, then stitch them to the wide Bargello strips. Just don't make the rectangles too narrow and drive yourself crazy!

◆ When constructing color runs, emphasize one color and make another one less dominant by changing the widths of the color-run strips.

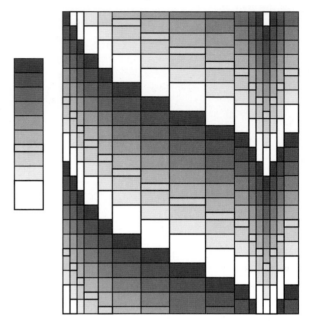

◆ Use a standard unit (1", for example), then vary the color-run strips by one-half the unit (½"), one-and-a-half or two times the unit (1½" or 2"), or other multiples of that unit. Develop a whole new look to your Bargello design by changing the color-run structure.

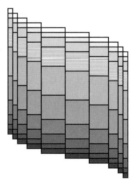

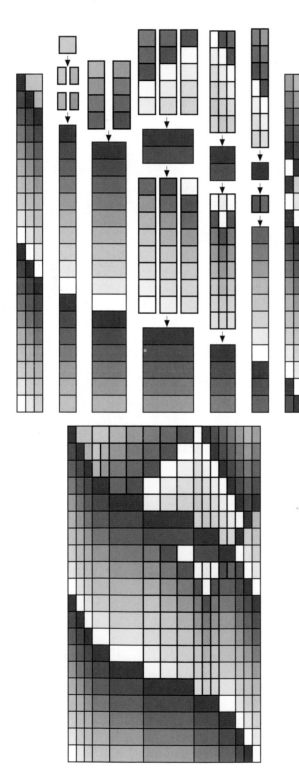

◆ Cut an odd number of Bargello strips, then arrange them symmetrically as shown below.

Join two of these symmetrical units end to end, reversing one set of Bargello strips as shown. Insert graduated widths of fabric at the center of the design, then add strips at the ends to create the illusion of background.

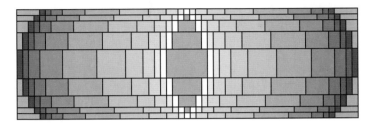

◆ Sewing a Log Cabin–type Bargello construction to the backing is a challenge, but the possibilities are certainly interesting. Vary the strips in your color run by units as directed on page 32. In the example below, the color run's two outer strips are each one unit wide, finished (¼"), the next block is two units wide (½"), the next is three units wide (¾"), etc. Cut the loops off the color run, following the same order of strip widths (¼", ½", ¾", etc.) used in the color-run strip. This method results in squares at each Bargello-strip intersection.

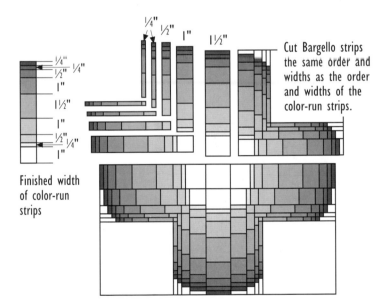

Finished width of color-run strips

Cut Bargello strips the same order and widths as the order and widths of the color-run strips.

Add background strips to the outer ends of the Bargello strips before they are sewn together, then cut squares for each corner of the log cabin (or fill in with other strip designs).

The "Margello" quilts are constructed on point, Log Cabin style, starting from a central square and working outward. The tube is built with strips of varying widths; then the loops are cut from the tubes in widths as directed

above. Note the horizontal row of on-point squares running through the center of the piece. See the color photos on pages 42 and 44.

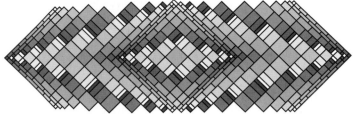

◆ Substitute segments of muted or darker versions of your fabrics or use the reverse side of a print in the main color run. Include groups of fabrics to create shadows or sunlit streaks in your original design. In the "Flower Garden" quilt on page 41, yellower versions of the fabrics in the original color run were substituted to give the appearance of beams of sunlight glowing across the quilt.

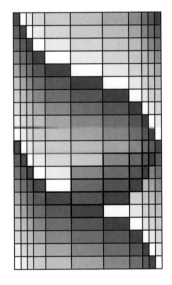 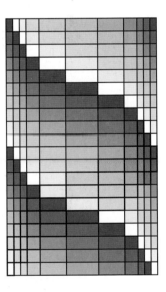

◆ Try replacing some of the large fabric blocks with traditional quilt squares.

◆ Use Bargello curves for a medallion quilt border. Notice that the corner squares are a challenge, but the effect is worth the work!

Creating Your Own Designs

Cutting strips from several different color runs instead of from just one tube allows more design freedom. However, it is important to sew the Bargello-strip sections together carefully to ensure precise widths. When working with Bargello strips cut from a tube, you can align the strips easily when stitching them together. If your design requires several color runs, take care to sew the strips accurately, or interchanging and stitching them together into the design will be tricky.

1. Before committing fabric to the design, use paper mock-ups to plan your quilt. Make several photocopies of the color-run paper printed on pages 92-94 and cut them into strips to use as practice Bargello strips. Cut off parts of strips by values or groups of "fabrics" if necessary to make your design. Photocopy the page of solid texture on page 95 to use as desired for large background areas or as solid separator strips.

2. Draw a curve on graph paper and block it out as instructed on page 13. Photocopy the grids on pages 89-91 and experiment with them to see which type you like best. You will paste your paper Bargello strips down onto this gridded paper as you finalize your design.

3. Using a rotary cutter with an old blade, cut off paper Bargello strips from the color-run paper to correspond to a segment of your graphed curve. Arrange these strips, moving them up and down as though you were designing in fabric. Cut them wide and narrow, depending upon the blocks on the graph. When you are satisfied with the progress, use some glue to stick them in place.

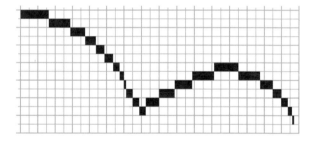

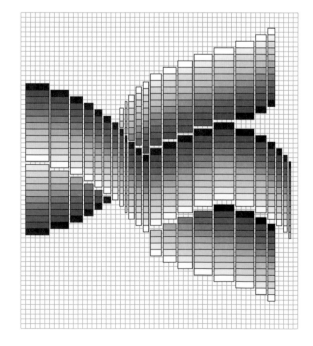

4. Play with contrasting curved lines and areas. Some of the curve design elements in your paper plan will use the entire length of the Bargello strip; others will use only sections of that strip. Place additional paper Bargello strips above or below the original curve structure.

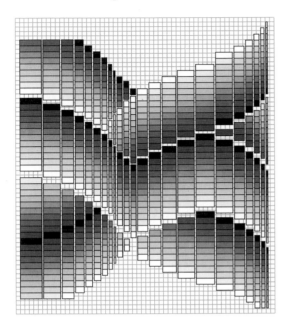

TIP: As you design with paper, don't be afraid to work on areas more than once. You may even need to start over with a clean piece of grid paper and a new photocopy of the color-run page. It is much easier to start over with paper than it is with fabric!

5. Continue experimenting with your paper design until you have constructed an actual image of the final piece. This is not a quick process, so be patient with yourself. Allow some inspiration to help guide your paper design. While the diagrams in this book offer many creative ideas, they do not begin to cover all the variations possible.

To keep sane, build the design on the structure that is dictated by the original graphed curve. Vary from this curve only if you decide to include wider or narrower vertical or horizontal sections (as in "Fireflies" on pages 72-76).

6. Once you have a picture of your project, it is time to cut fabric! Using nine to fifteen fabrics, cut and sew a few color runs from them, but do not sew them into tubes unless the design calls for them. The number of color runs needed is hard to predict since you will frequently incorporate short segments of Bargello strips into the design.

N O T E

For the fabric version of your design, choose a large rectangle of flannel or fleece to use as a design wall.

7. As you cut the first strip off the color run, pin it onto the design wall in the appropriate location and work from that point. As with simpler projects, start from the center Bargello strips and work to the outer edges.

8. Cut and pin Bargello strips across the basic curve and then work on some of the embellishment areas. You may decide to replace segments of your original Bargello strips with strips that form a secondary design. At the point on the original strip where the new strip begins, open the seam, remove the unneeded portion of the strip, and insert the new section of Bargello to match your paper pattern. Take care to sew precise ¼" seams so your color runs match easily when they are sewn together.

TIP: As you replace some segments of your Bargello strips, do not throw away the section you removed. Use these short lengths in another part of your project. It is nice to plan for that to happen if you are a frugal quilter like I am! You will not be able to predict every design possibility on your paper plan, but do try to plan as much as possible.

TIP: Locate your design wall so you can step back and see how the plan is working out. Or, use a reducing tool to see the overall effect of your design. As you pin strips to the wall, you may see changes you want to make in the Bargello strips. This is the time to remove and replace segments until the effect is just what you want.

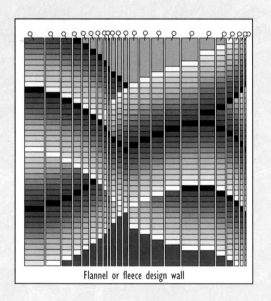

Flannel or fleece design wall

9. Before you begin sewing strips, you must be certain the design is what you want. If you sew the strips too early and later change your mind about the quilt plan, it will be difficult (and tedious) to undo your work. The paper plan is so important; if you like the design, and it uses many exciting Bargello elements, the fabric rendition will fall into place. Once you are satisfied with the design, sew down the first Bargello strips.

Construct the quilt as described in the "Basic Bargello Instruction" section on pages 10–24. Consider, however, adding more striking borders than suggested in that section. Maybe some of your Bargello wants to extend out of bounds, as suggested at the top and bottom of "Fractured Rhapsody" on page 84. Refer to "Bye-bye Blues" on page 65, where the blue-to-brown idea carries over into the pieced borders. Asymmetric finishes are perhaps a more logical addition to off-balance designs than straightforward strip borders. In addition, consider varying the width of the border strips. This may even be a good time to add a fabric or color that isn't in your color runs but coordinates well.

With the tools and techniques you have learned from all this experimenting, you should be well on your way to creating an exciting, one-of-a-kind work of art.

Good quilting!

Gallery

Emerald Isle

By Marge Edie, 1990, Clemson, South Carolina, 44" x 55". My first Bargello project was this wedding/Christmas gift for my brother and his bride. (Collection of Steve Clements and Brooke Greiner)

Christmas Throw

By Marge Edie, 1992, Clemson, South Carolina, 50" x 69". The many beautiful Christmas prints available today blend well in Bargello designs. (Collection of Fred and Bonnie Edie)

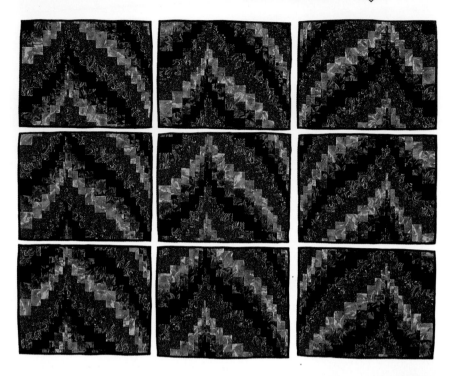

Nine Early Autumn Place Mats

By Marge Edie, 1993, Clemson, South Carolina, each 13⅜" x 17". I made these to match our every-day dishes and to tie in with the outdoor view from our table.

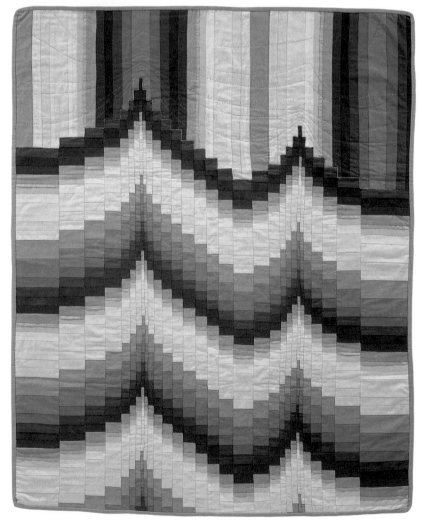

Explosion in Spring

By Betsy Hegg, 1991, Clemson, South Carolina, 38½" x 49¼". To select the fabrics for this quilt, Betsy chose colors from a floral oil painting done by her talented mother. Both the painting and the quilt are focal points in her living area.

Aurora Borealis

By Erika T. Meriwether, 1993, Clemson, South Carolina, 50" x 38". Erika's husband is a physicist whose specialty is the northern lights. With a video for reference, she carefully studied the colors and patterns of the aurora borealis to create this work of art for his office.

Persian Nights

By Mary Laib, 1993, Seneca, South Carolina, 60" x 30". When Mary redecorated her bedroom, she made this wall hanging to place over the bed, choosing colors to match her Oriental rug and new wallpaper border.

Teal We Meet

By Mary Sullivan, 1993, Seneca, South Carolina, 52" x 43". Mary made this in a beginning Bargello class. We all loved her gentle colors.

To the Sea... the Coral Sea

By Marge Edie, 1991, Clemson, South Carolina, 106" x 106". The song "Sea of Love" ran through my head during part of this construction. Since Jennifer Amor started me on the long Bargello road, I named this quilt with her in mind.

Flower Garden

By Marge Edie, 1993, Clemson, South Carolina, 38¾" x 53¼". By using yellowed versions of the surrounding colors in the quilt, I created the look of sunbeams drifting across the piece.

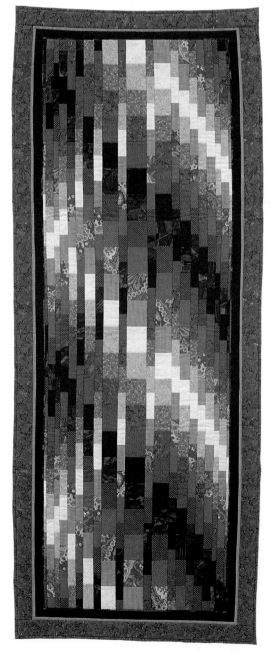

Ups and Downs

By Marge Edie, 1993, Clemson, South Carolina, 23¾" x 62½". A wide variety of fabrics were used here, from the traditional to the reckless, with many formal textures in between.

Margello Sand

By Marge Edie, 1993, Clemson, South Carolina, 22" x 63". This was the original "Margello" quilt, envisioned by my husband for our living room. We chose the colors for that location.

Miami Skyline

By Marge Edie, 1993, Clemson, South Carolina, 40½" x 57". The citrus colors and horizontal reflection suggested the name for this quilt.

Painted Desert Sunrise

By Marge Edie, 1993, Clemson, South Carolina, 22¼" x 51¼". Peaches, golds, and blues, the colors in sand and sky, remind me of the Southwest we visited when I was young.

Through a Glass Darkly

By Marge Edie, 1994, Clemson, South Carolina, 38⅞" x 29½". This variation of "Underwater Reflections" features "borders" created by rectangles of fabric added to the Bargello strips on a strip-by-strip basis. The possibilities of design enhancement using the "Reflections" structure are endless.

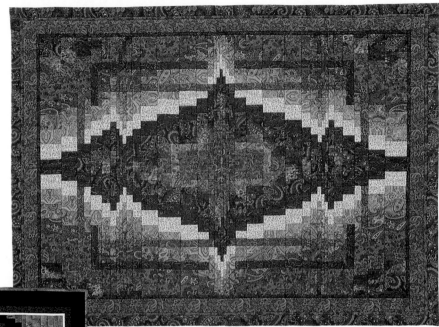

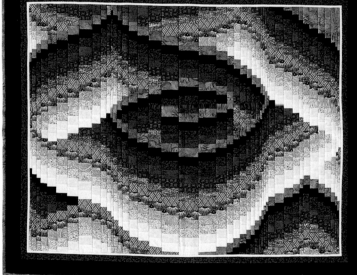

Hurricane Georg

By Georgia Schmidt, 1993, Lake Jackson, Texas, 40" x 33". Georgia was a student in my first advanced Bargello quilt class and this was her class project! Her talent and ability to manipulate the curves amazed us all.

Point of No Return

By Georgia Schmidt, 1993, Lake Jackson, Texas, 37" x 49". Heat appears to glow inside the ribbon arrangement. The black background augments the colors of the ribbon, creating more intensity and adding drama to the quilt.

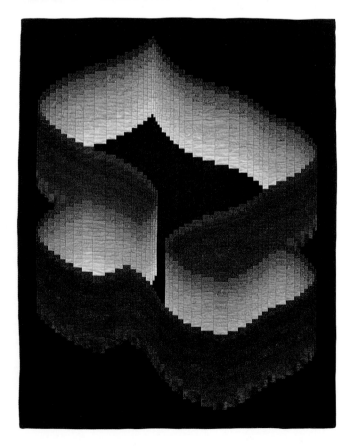

Garnet Glory

By Marge Edie, 1994, Clemson, South Carolina, 22³/₈" x 60³/₈". This "Margello" variation uses 12 different fabrics and incorporates leftover tube segments in the borders.

Sweet April Rain

By Marge Edie, 1994, Clemson, South Carolina, 46" x 37⁵/₈". The easiest way to check my pattern instructions for "Fractured Rhapsody" was to re-create the quilt. However, the rainy feel is more striking when this piece is hung upside down.

Crayon Wash

By Marge Edie, 1994, Clemson, South Carolina, 51¹/₂" x 50¹/₂". In this variation of "Bye-bye Blues," I split the loops in different locations for a slight change from the original pattern. The title is a take-off on the wonderful colourwash quilts, since these crayon-box colors fade to pastels on the right side of the piece.

The Patterns

The following directions are based on using 42"- to 44"-wide, 100% cotton fabric and ¼"-wide seam allowances. Refer to construction techniques in the "Basic Bargello Instruction" section on pages 10–24. Measurements given are for cut sizes.

These patterns begin with the easiest project, Purple Fanfare Place Mats. Practice the Quilt-As-You-Build-It construction method with the easy place mats first to prepare you for making any of the other Bargello variations. The patterns following the place mats vary in their level of difficulty, as indicated with each pattern.

Purple Fanfare Place Mats

By Marge Edie, 1990, Clemson, South Carolina, 17" x 13³⁄₈", 3 of 6 shown.

These are Clemson University's colors—I just had to include them in a project for this book.

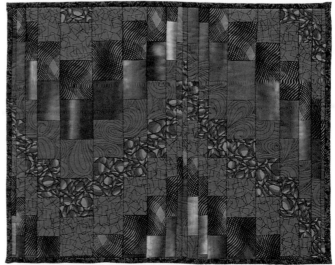

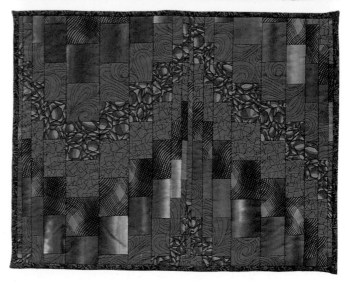

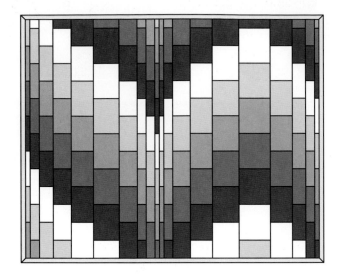

2. Sew 4 of the color runs together into a tube.

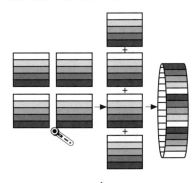

3. Cut the other 2 color runs in half and stitch together to make 1 half-size tube as shown.

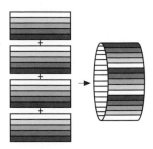

This set of six place mats is quick to make and will provide the step-by-step experience necessary to complete larger and more complicated Bargello quilts. Since a place mat is smaller than a full-size quilt, you will only need to use five different colors for a spectacular finished effect. Make the place mats casual or formal. Choose fabrics to coordinate with colors in your kitchen or dining room or to match your china.

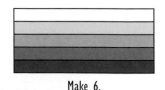

Materials

44"-wide fabric

$\frac{1}{2}$ yd. *each* of 5 colors
$1\frac{1}{4}$ yds. for backing
40" x 42" rectangle of batting
$\frac{1}{2}$ yd. for binding

Directions

1. Cut 6 strips, each $2\frac{1}{2}$" wide, from each fabric. Construct 6 color runs.

Make 6.

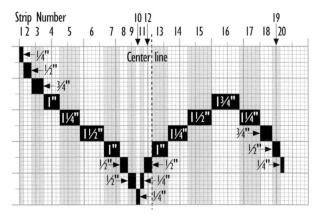

N O T E

For Bargello strips, cut two sets of loops from the tubes, referring to the chart on page 47 for strip width and quantity. Cut off each loop as you need it or cut all the loops at once and label each with its strip number as you cut it from the tube. Each set of twenty Bargello strips will be sewn onto a 20"-wide prepared rectangle of batting and backing. These two "quilts" will then be cut into three place mats each.

Refer to the graph below and the chart on page 47 for placement and width of strips. When placing each Bargello strip, refer to the graph to see whether the curve moves up or down.

Grid squares equal $\frac{1}{4}$". Measurements given are for *finished* strip widths.

Strip #	No. of Strips Per Set	Cut Strip Width	Finished Strip Width
1, 10, 11, 20	4	3/4"	1/4"
2, 8, 9, 12, 19	5	1"	1/2"
3, 18	2	1 1/4"	3/4"
4, 7, 13	3	1 1/2"	1"
5, 14, 17	3	1 3/4"	1 1/4"
6, 15	2	2"	1 1/2"
16	1	2 1/4"	1 3/4"

Assembling the Quilt

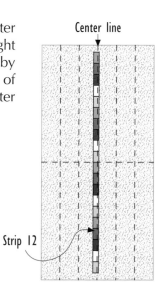

NOTE

Directions are given for constructing one "quilt" that will be cut into three place mats. Repeat steps 1–8 for the second "quilt."

1. From the backing fabric, cut two 20"-wide strips from selvage to selvage. Cut the batting into 2 rectangles, each 20" x 42". Prepare the backing and batting, following the directions given in "Preparing the Backing and Batting" on pages 14-15.

2. Cut a 1"-wide loop from the tube for Strip 12. Select the fabric rectangle you want to place at the top of the strip. Remove the stitching at the top of this rectangle as shown.

3. Place Strip 12 along the center line, right side up, with the right edge overlapping the center line by 1/4" as shown. Align the center of the strip with the horizontal center line. Pin each fabric rectangle.

Center line

Strip 12

4. For Strip 13, cut across the loop at the center of the rectangle that matches Strip 12's top rectangle. (For sewing staggered seams, see page 16 of "Sewing the Bargello Strips.")

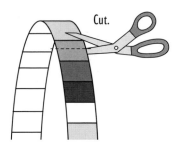

Cut.

5. Place Strip 13 on top of Strip 12, right sides together, matching edges along the right side. Align the cut edge of Strip 13's top and bottom rectangles with the pulled-out seam line of Strip 12's top and bottom rectangles as shown.

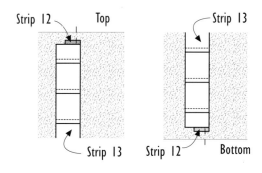

Strip 12   Top   Strip 13

Strip 13   Strip 12   Bottom

6. Pin in place, then stitch with a 1/4"-wide seam allowance along the right edges of the strips. Flip Strip 13 to the side and press if necessary.

7. Remove the stitching from the top rectangle of Strip 14. Place Strip 14 on top of Strip 13 with right sides together. Pin in place and stitch. Flip and press to the side.

8. Stitch Strips 15–20 to the quilt, sewing strips across the quilt to the right side. Refer to the graph on page 46 and the chart above left for strip widths and placement.

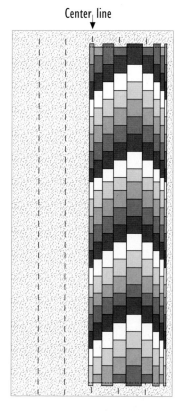

Center line

9. For Strip 11, cut across the loop at the center of the rectangle that matches the bottom rectangle of Strip 12. Place Strip 11 on top of Strip 12 with right sides together, matching edges along the left side. Align the cut edge of the top and bottom rectangle with the pulled-out seam line of Strip 12's top and bottom rectangles. Pin and stitch to the quilt through the backing and batting. Press Strip 13 to the side.

Binding

1. From binding fabric, cut 10 strips, each $1\frac{1}{4}$" wide, from selvage to selvage. Join ends with 45°-angle seams as needed.

2. Bind, following the directions for $\frac{1}{4}$", single-thickness binding in "Borders and Binding" on pages 21-24.

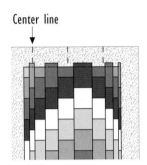

Center line

10. Stitch Strips 10–1 to the quilt, sewing strips and staggering seam lines across the quilt to the left side. Refer to the graph on page 46 and the chart on page 47 for strip widths and placement.

11. When all the Bargello strips are sewn in place, baste along the right and left edges to hold Strips 1 and 20 in place. Trim the uneven edges along the top and bottom and trim excess from each side. Cut across the quilt to make three place mats as shown at right, each measuring approximately $13\frac{3}{8}$" x 17". Repeat for the other three place mats.

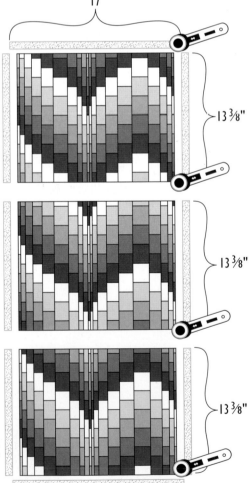

17"

$13\frac{3}{8}$"

$13\frac{3}{8}$"

$13\frac{3}{8}$"

Moonlight and Roses

By Marge Edie, 1993, Clemson, South Carolina, 38¹/₂" x 54". Interesting patterns occur when two different Bargello curves unite. The contrast and the colors resemble romance—sometimes soft, sometimes vivid.

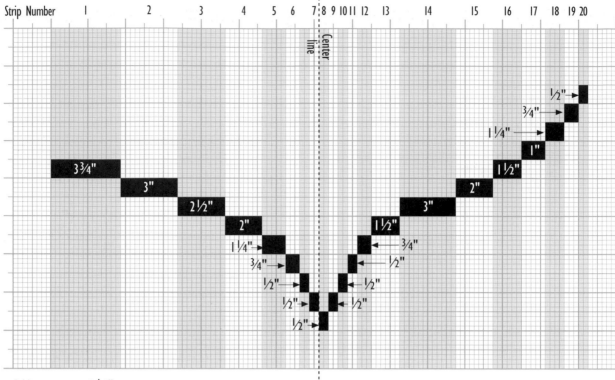

Strip Number

3¾" 3" 2½" 2" 1¼"→ ¾"→ ½"→ ½"→ ½"→ ½" ½" ½" ¾" 1½" 3" 2" 1½" 1" 1¼" ¾" ½"

Center line

Grid squares equal ¼".

Measurements given are for *finished* strip widths.

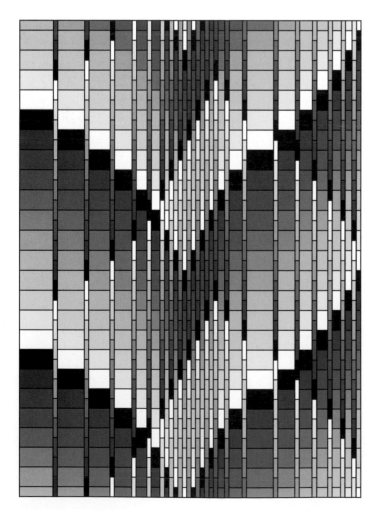

U se separator strips to dramatically enhance the simplest Bargello curve design and add visual complexity to the project. Choose solid fabric strips for separators as shown in "Fractured Rhapsody" on page 84 or cut strips from leftover or new color runs. The separator strips in this pattern are cut from the same tubes as the main curve design.

When you make contrasting curves with separator strips, the results can be difficult to predict. Arrange strips several different ways on the design wall before stitching. See "Separator Strips" on page 28.

Materials

44"-wide fabric

⅜ yd. each of 12 colors
⅛ yd. for inner border
¼ yd. for outer border
3 yds. for backing
48" x 64" rectangle of batting
½ yd. for binding

Directions

1. Cut 3 strips, each 2¾" wide, from each of the 12 colors. Construct 3 color runs.

Make 3.

2. Sew 2 color runs into a tube. Cut the third color run in half and stitch together to make one half-size tube as shown.

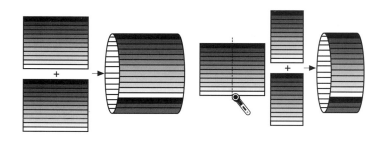

3. Refer to the charts below and at right for placement and width of strips for the main Bargello design. When placing each Bargello strip, refer to the graph on page 50 to see whether the curve moves up or down.

Strip #	No. of Strips	Cut Strip Width	Finished Strip Width
7–12, 21	7	1"	½"
6, 13, 20	3	1¼"	¾"
19	1	1½"	1"
5, 18	2	1¾"	1¼"
14, 17	2	2"	1½"
4, 16	2	2½"	2"
3	1	3"	2½"
2, 15	2	3½"	3"
1	1	4¼"	3¾"

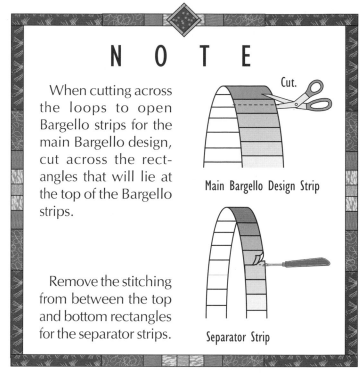

NOTE

When cutting across the loops to open Bargello strips for the main Bargello design, cut across the rectangles that will lie at the top of the Bargello strips.

Main Bargello Design Strip

Remove the stitching from between the top and bottom rectangles for the separator strips.

Separator Strip

4. Arrange the main Bargello design strips on the design wall.

5. Cut 20 separator strips, each 1" wide, from the tube.

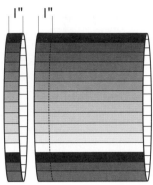

6. Open the loop by removing the stitching from the top rectangle. (See note on page 51.) Set in the separator strips between the main Bargello strips in the arrangement of your choice.

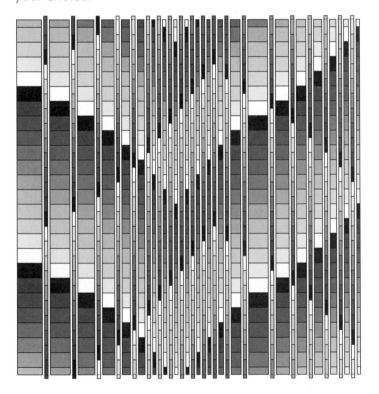

7. Prepare backing and batting, following directions in "Preparing the Backing and Batting" on pages 14-15.

8. Place Strip 8 along the center line and place a separator strip on top, right sides together. Following the directions on page 16 for staggered seams, align the right edges of the strips. Pin, then stitch, with 1/4"-wide seam allowances, along the right sides of the strips. Flip the separator strip over and press if necessary. Continue sewing the Bargello strips and separator strips, working across to Strip 21 at the right edge of the quilt. Refer to the directions given for "Sewing the Bargello Strips" on pages 16-21.

9. Sew strips from the center to the left side of the quilt, alternating separator strips with Strips 1–7.

Borders and Binding

1. From inner border fabric, cut 5 strips, each 3/4" wide. Join strips as needed. Following the directions for "Borders" on page 21–22, sew side borders to the quilt, then add top and bottom borders.

2. From outer border fabric, cut 5 strips, each 1 3/4" wide. Join strips as needed and sew borders to quilt, following the directions in step 1. To maintain an even 1/4"-wide inner border, sew each outer border from the back. (See tips for sewing uniform seams from the back on page 20.)

3. Trim away batting and backing, leaving about 7/8" extending beyond the edge of the outer border.

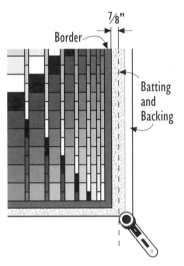

4. From binding fabric, cut 5 strips, each 2 3/4" wide. Join ends as needed with a 45°-angle seam. Follow directions for single-thickness binding given in "Binding" on pages 23-24. The binding will measure 1 1/8" wide when finished.

Underwater Reflections

By Marge Edie, 1993, Clemson, South Carolina, 39 x 30¼". The magenta contrasting curve pattern adds interest to an otherwise formally structured quilt.

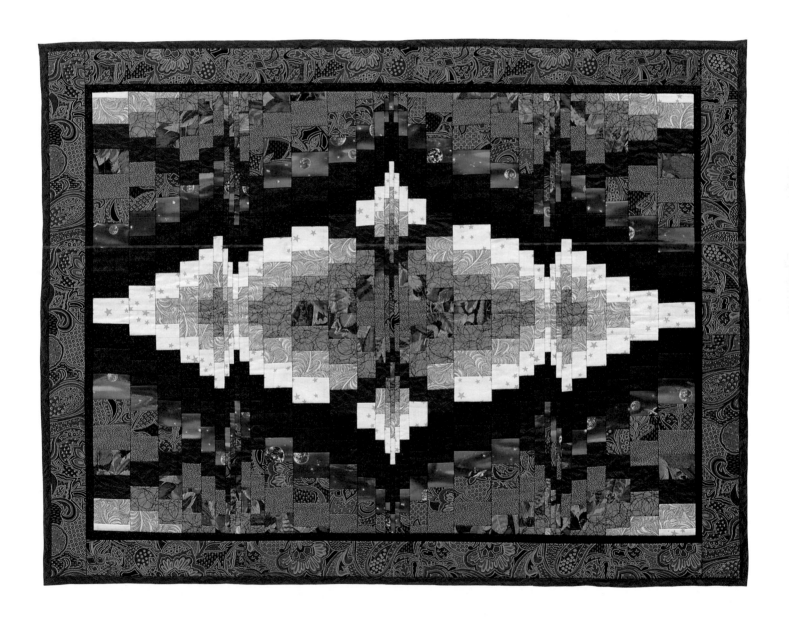

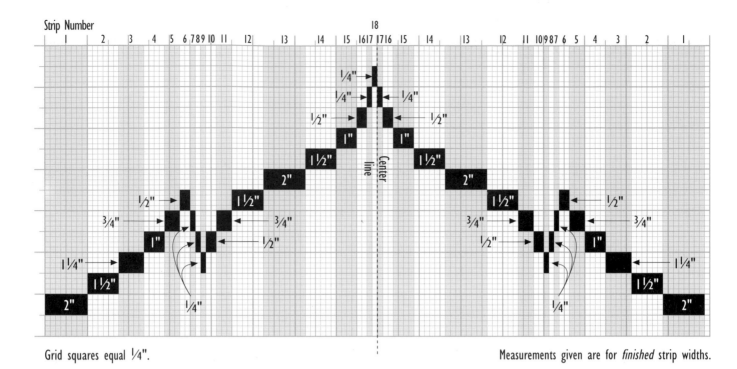

Strip Number

Grid squares equal ¼".

Measurements given are for *finished* strip widths.

Materials

44"-wide fabric

¼ yd. each of 9 colors
¼ yd. of contrasting color
¼ yd. for inner border
⅜ yd. for outer border
1 yd. for backing
36" x 45" rectangle of batting
¼ yd. for binding

This attractive design is easier to make than it looks at first glance. Learn just two tricks, then complete the quilt rapidly.

Make the quilt as directed by substituting some of the regular Bargello rectangles with contrasting fabric. You can, however, make a reflection quilt without these contrasting curve lines.

"Miami Skyline" on page 42 uses the same graph as this quilt, but the contrast is reversed (with a dark central motif instead of a dark background) and the color run strips are cut twice the width of those in "Underwater Reflections." There are no contrasting curve lines in "Miami Skyline," and the fabrics feature more subdued textures.

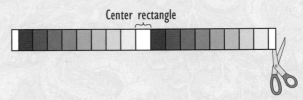

Directions

1. From each of 9 colors, cut 3 strips, each 1⅞" wide. Sew the strips together to make 3 color runs.

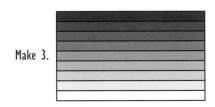

Make 3.

2. Use 2 of the color runs to make 1 tube. Cut the third color run in half and create 1 half-size tube.

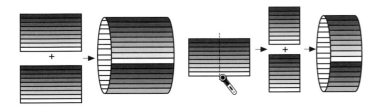

3. From the contrasting fabric, cut 3 strips, each 1⅞" wide, for the contrasting curve line.

4. Referring to the graph on page 54 and the chart below, cut loops from the tubes. When placing each Bargello strip, refer to the graph to see whether the curve moves up or down. (For each strip number below, cut 2 loops, 1 for the left side of the quilt, and 1 for the right side. Cut only 1 loop for center Strip 18.)

Strip # (L and R)	No. of Strips	Cut Strip Width	Finished Strip Width
7, 8, 9, 17, 18*	9	¾"	¼"
6, 10, 16	6	1"	½"
5, 11	4	1¼"	¾"
4, 15	4	1½"	1"
3	2	1¾"	1¼"
2, 12, 14	6	2"	1½"
1, 13	4	2½"	2"

*Cut 1 for Strip 18.

5. Open each loop and resew it in one of two ways, according to the strip's placement on the quilt. Alternate the two techniques (explained in the box at right) across the quilt. Use Method 2 for the center strip (#18), then Method 1 for the next strip, and repeat this sequence to the edge of the quilt.

Method 1

1. For each strip, find the center rectangle of the loop. To open the loop, cut across the rectangle of matching fabric in the loop's second color run.

Center rectangle

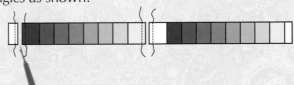

2. Remove stitches from the center and outer rectangles as shown.

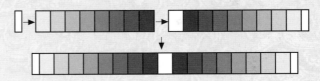

3. Reverse the separated section and resew to the strip. Resew the removed partial rectangle to the end of the strip, as shown.

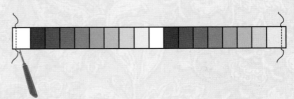

Method 2

1. For each strip, find the center rectangle of the loop. To open the loop, remove the stitching in the seam at the top of the matching rectangle in the strip's second color run.

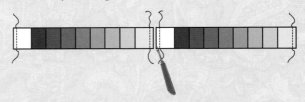

2. Remove the stitching from the center rectangle as shown, separating the color-run strips.

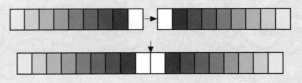

3. Reverse the separated section and resew to the strip.

6. After you have resewn a Bargello strip, place it on the design wall to ensure that you have assembled the strips correctly.

7. Following the diagram below, substitute contrasting fabric segments into the design. Carefully pull out the stitching between rectangles.

8. Discard the removed rectangle and substitute a contrasting rectangle of the same size, cut from the 1⅞"-wide strip. Resew the strip together, matching ¼"-wide seams to maintain the rectangles' dimensions.

9. Prepare backing and batting according to directions in "Preparing the Backing and Batting" on pages 14-15.

10. Place Strip 18 along the center line of the batting and backing. Place strip 17R on top of Strip 18, right sides together. Align right edges in a staggered seam arrangement. (See directions for staggered seams in "Sewing the Bargello Strips" on page 16.) Stitch along the right edge with a ¼"-wide seam allowance. Flip Strip 17R to the right and press if necessary.

11. Continue sewing strips to the quilt, working from the center to the right side. (See "Sewing the Bargello Strips" on pages 16-21.)

12. Stitch Strip 17L to Strip 18, then continue sewing strips to the quilt, working from the center to the left side.

Borders and Binding

1. From inner border fabric, cut 4 strips, each ⅞" wide. Following the directions for "Borders" on pages 21-22, measure, cut, and stitch side borders to the quilt. Repeat for top and bottom borders.

2. From outer border fabric, cut 4 strips, each 2½" wide. Add borders, repeating step 1 above.

3. Trim away batting and backing, leaving about ¼" extending beyond the edge of the outer border.

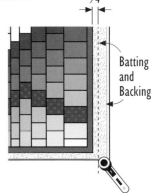

Batting and Backing

4. From binding fabric, cut 4 strips, each 1½" wide. Sew ends together with 45°-angle seams as needed. Follow directions for single-thickness binding in "Binding" on pages 23-24. The binding will measure ½" wide when finished.

These 4 Bargello strips are not changed.

Margello Blue

By Marge Edie, 1993, Clemson, South Carolina, 19" x 63". The "Margello" technique creates sparkle and depth with a minimum of difficulty. Based on Log Cabin construction, it differs from the traditional flame-point Bargello structure.

his design resulted when my husband helped me create a wall hanging that wasn't in the typical Bargello flame-point style for our living room. We spent time trying to invent something with a diagonal orientation and, as a team, came up with this design, which Dan named after me. The original "Margello," seen on page 42, varies slightly from the instructions for this quilt. Although this quilt doesn't have the traditional Bargello curves, the construction method is nearly identical.

The width of the wall hanging depends upon the length of the color run. More fabrics or wider fabric strips in the color runs create more width for the quilt.

Notice that squares form where two adjacent "Margello" strips meet. The squares' color order is the same order in which they are sewn into the Margello strips. As subsequent Margello strips are sewn in place, each color, for example strip 6, moves closer to the square's position. The sides of each square equal the width of the color-run strip cut from the square's fabric. If you wish to feature large squares of particular fabrics or colors, plan to use those fabrics for the wide color-run strips.

Materials

44"-wide fabric

¼ yd. *each* of 3 dominant colors for colors 1, 2, and 11
¼ yd. *each* of 5 medium-value colors for colors 3, 4, 5, 9, and 10
¼ yd. *each* of 3 contrasting colors for colors 6, 7, and 8
⅜ yd. *each* of 2 fabrics for edge strips and triangles
⅛ yd. for inner borders
⅛ yd. for outer borders
2 yds. for backing
22" x 66" rectangle of batting
¼ yd. for binding

Directions

Constructing Color Runs

1. Arrange fabrics so the dominant fabrics will be cut as wide strips and the contrasting fabrics cut as narrow strips. Cut 3 strips from each fabric, referring to the chart below.

Fabric #	Strip Width	Finished Strip Width
1	2¼"	1¾"
2, 11	2"	1½"
3	1¾"	1¼"
4, 10	1½"	1"
5, 9	1¼"	¾"
6, 8	1"	½"
7	¾"	¼"

2. Make a color map by gluing a scrap of each fabric on a large index card. Mark each fabric with its number and its corresponding strip width.

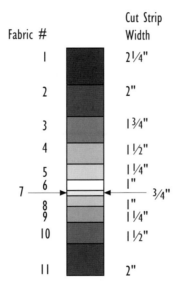

Fabric #		Cut Strip Width
1		2¼"
2		2"
3		1¾"
4		1½"
5		1¼"
6		1"
7	→	¾"
8		1"
9		1¼"
10		1½"
11		2"

3. Sew the color-run strips into 3 color runs of 11 fabric strips each.

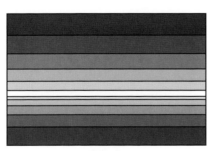

Make 3.

4. Sew 2 of the color runs into a tube. Cut the other color run in half and sew the 2 halves together to make one half-size tube.

Assembling the Quilt

1. Cut the backing fabric to measure 22" x 66". Layer the backing and batting, pin them together with safety pins, then draw horizontal and vertical center lines.

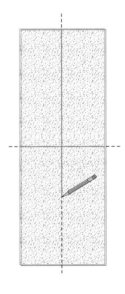

2. Draw a vertical line 10" to the left and 10" to the right of the center vertical line.

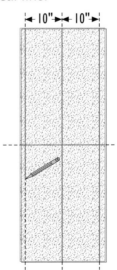

3. Align the 45°-angle mark of a cutting guide with the vertical center line. Draw diagonal lines about 6" apart. Use these lines as guides to keep your Margello design aligned correctly.

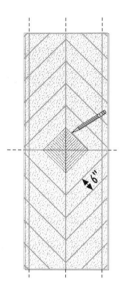

4. Cut a 4¾" x 4¾" center square. Use one fabric or piece it if you wish. For a pieced square, cut 2 squares, each 5½" x 5½". Cut each square in half twice diagonally.

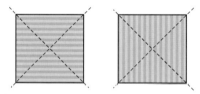

5. Combine quarters to create the interwoven pattern as shown. Stitch quarters, then halves together. The square should measure 4¾" x 4¾". You will have 4 quarters remaining to use for another project.

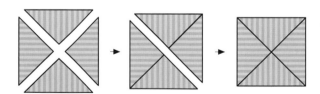

6. Pin the square diagonally in place over the center intersection of the vertical and horizontal lines, placing corners on the pencil lines as shown.

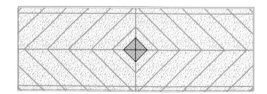

7. Cut 2 loops from the tube, each 1¼" wide. Pull out the stitches and remove Fabrics 3–8 as shown. Reserve these partial strips. Use only the part that includes Fabrics 9–11,1, and 2. You will have 4 short "Margello" strips.

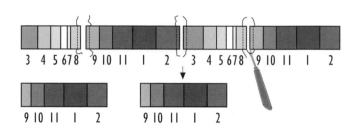

8. From 2 of the Margello strips, remove Fabrics 2 and 9.

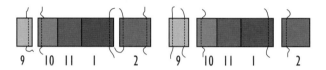

9. Sew the 2 shortest Margello strips onto the upper left and lower right sides of the center square as shown, stitching through the batting and backing. Pull the thread ends through to the front side and knot them. Flip the Margello strips outward from the center square, press if necessary, and pin them down securely.

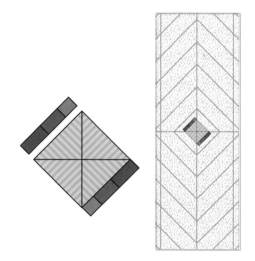

10. Sew the 2 longer Margello strips onto the lower left and upper right sides of the center square and across the ends of the 2 previous strips. Pin the outer square's seam lines to line up with the strips and trim any excess fabric at the left and right sides. Pull the thread ends to the front, knot them, flip, press if necessary, and pin.

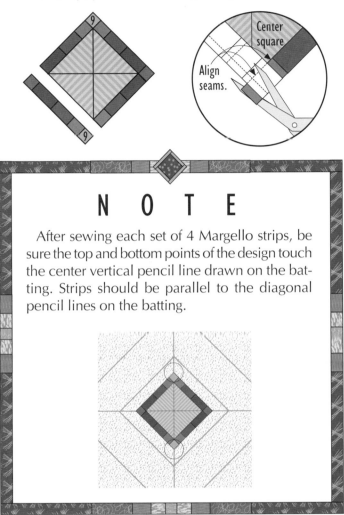

NOTE

After sewing each set of 4 Margello strips, be sure the top and bottom points of the design touch the center vertical pencil line drawn on the batting. Strips should be parallel to the diagonal pencil lines on the batting.

11. Cut off 2 loops, each 1½" wide, from the tube. Pull out the stitches to remove Fabrics 5–9. Reserve these partial strips. Use only the part that includes Fabrics 10–11 and 1–4. You will have 4 Margello strips.

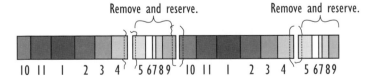

12. From 2 of these strips, remove Fabrics 10 and 4.

13. Sew the 2 shortest Margello strips onto the upper left and lower right sides of the center square and previous strip ends, trimming off excess fabric if necessary. Pull threads through to the front, flip, press, and pin.

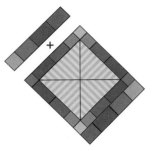

14. Sew the longer Margello strips to the square, repeating step 10.

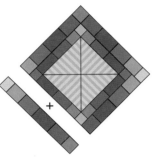

15. Cut off 2 loops, each 2" wide, from the tube and remove Fabric 10. From 2 of the Margello strips, remove Fabric 11.

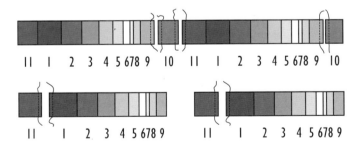

16. Sew the 2 shorter Margello strips onto the upper left and lower right sides of the center square and across the previous strip ends, trimming off excess fabric if necessary. Stitch, pull threads through, flip, press, and pin.

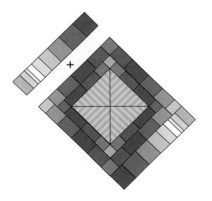

17. Before sewing the next 2 Margello strips, cut 2 new 2" squares of Fabric 10. Replace each strip's shorter Fabric 10 rectangle with a new square so that each strip will align with the end of the strips sewn in step 18.

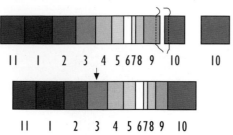

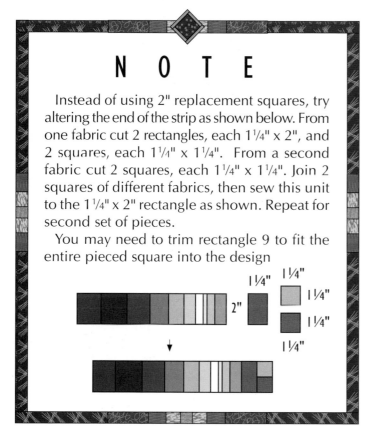

18. Sew the altered Margello strips onto the lower left and upper right sides of the center square. Pull the threads through, flip, press, and pin.

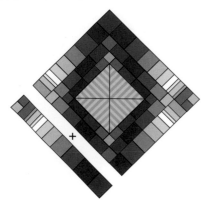

Adding Setting Triangles and Strips

1. For the next 9 sets of 4 Margello strips, add a triangle to each outer edge before sewing the strip down. Use the same fabric for every outer triangle, choose one color for the triangles at the quilt's upper half and another color for the quilt's lower half, or use the fabric that would appear next in each Margello strip.

Make 4 triangles by cutting a square in half twice diagonally. Refer to the chart below for the size to cut. Triangles cut from these squares may be larger than necessary but should be trimmed later.

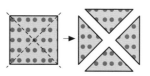

Strip Width	Size of Square
2¼"	3⅛"
2"	2⅞"
1¾"	2⅝"
1½"	2⅜"
1¼"	2⅛"
1"	1⅞"
¾"	1⅝"

2. Sew a short side of a triangle to the outer end of each Margello strip as shown.

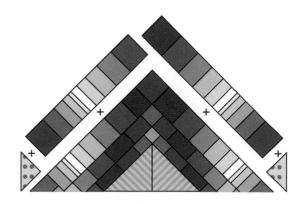

3. Cut strips, add triangles, and sew the 9 sets of Margello strips to upper and lower halves of the quilt.

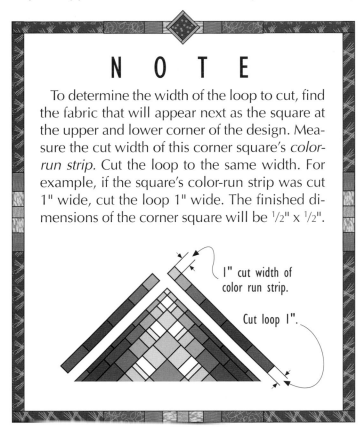

N O T E

To determine the width of the loop to cut, find the fabric that will appear next as the square at the upper and lower corner of the design. Measure the cut width of this corner square's *color-run strip.* Cut the loop to the same width. For example, if the square's color-run strip was cut 1" wide, cut the loop 1" wide. The finished dimensions of the corner square will be ½" x ½".

I" cut width of color run strip.

Cut loop I".

For each set of 2 Margello strips, remove a fabric rectangle from 1 of the strips, at the end that will be placed at the center of the quilt as shown. The matching fabric rectangle on the second strip will become the corner square.

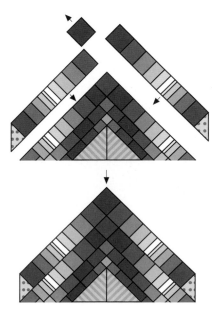

4. Each of the remaining 5 sets of Margello strips must gradually be made shorter to complete the design as it works its way to the top and bottom of the quilt. You may be able to use the partial strips you reserved in steps 7 and 11 on pages 60–61.

5. From the same fabric that you used for the edge triangles, cut strips and sew to the outer ends of the Margello strips. Cut each fill-in strip the same width as its Margello strip and long enough to reach the edge of the quilt.

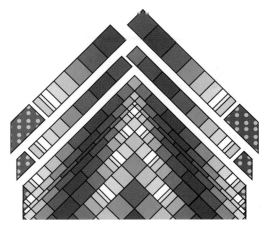

6. For the corners, cut 2 squares, each 7¼" x 7¼", from the edge-triangle fabric. Cut each square in half once diagonally.

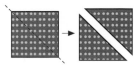

Sew the long edge of a triangle to each corner of the quilt. If you use a different fabric for each end of the quilt, cut one 7¼" square from each fabric.

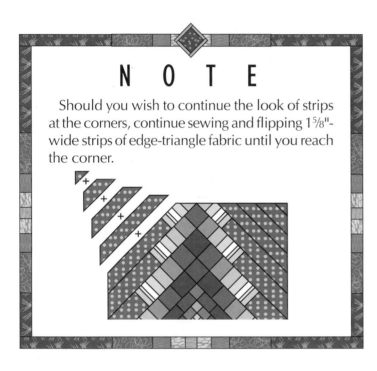

NOTE

Should you wish to continue the look of strips at the corners, continue sewing and flipping 1⅝"-wide strips of edge-triangle fabric until you reach the corner.

Borders and Binding

1. Square up the quilt by placing a cutting guide at the corner and marking the edges of the quilt. Do not cut along this line; use it only as a guide for border placement.

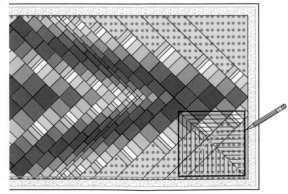

2. From inner border fabric, cut 4 strips, each ¾" wide. Following the directions for "Borders " on pages 21-22, measure, cut and stitch side borders to the quilt. Repeat for top and bottom borders.

3. From outer border fabric, cut 4 strips, each ⅝" wide. (This border's finished measurement is ⅛".) Measure quilt from top to bottom through the center and cut the side borders to this measurement. Pin the borders to the quilt and stitch from the back as directed in "Sewing the Bargello Strips" on pages 16-21. Sew side borders to the quilt.

4. Measure the quilt from side to side and repeat step 3 for top and bottom borders.

5. Trim away batting and backing, leaving ⅜" extending beyond the edge of the outer border.

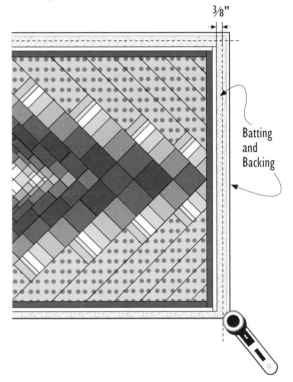

6. From binding fabric, cut 4 strips, each 1¾" wide. Sew ends together with 45°-angle seams as needed. Bind, following the directions for single-thickness binding in "Binding" on pages 23-24. Be very careful to maintain the ⅛" outer-border width all the way around the quilt. The binding will measure ⅝" wide when finished.

Bye-Bye Blues

By Marge Edie, 1993, Clemson, South Carolina, 52" x 52". By exchanging color-run strips during quilt construction, blue hues metamorphose into browns across the quilt from side to side.

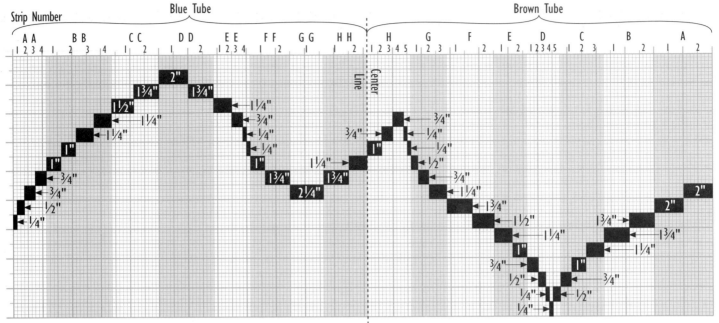

Strip Number

Blue Tube | Brown Tube

A A | B B | C C | D D | E E | F F | G G | H H | H | G | F | E | D | C | B | A

Center Line

2"
1¾" 1¾"
1½" 1¼"
1¼" 1¼" ¾" ¾"
1" ¼" ¾" ¼"
¾" ¼" 1" ¼"
½" 1" 1¼" 1" ½"
¼" 1¾" 1¾" ¾" 2"
2¼" ¾" 2"
1¼" 1¾" 1½" 1¾"
1" 1¼" 1¼" 1"
¾" ¾"
½" 1" ¾"
¼" ½"
¼"

Grid squares equal ¼".

Measurements given are for *finished* strip widths.

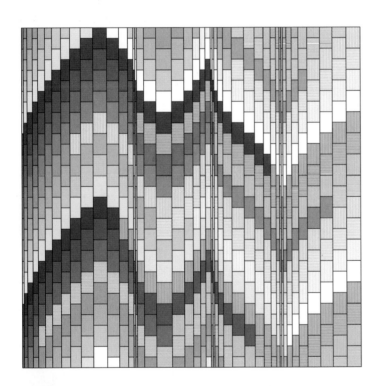

I n this quilt I tried to change colors as the Bargello curves moved across the quilt. The method given accomplishes this metamorphosis efficiently with a minimum of difficulty.

Experiment by making this quilt in other color ways. Choose rainbow colors, as in "Crayon Wash" on page 44, or start with solids on one side and gradually blend to prints on the other. Try dark colors on the left side and move to pastel versions of the same colors on the right.

Materials

44"-wide fabric

¼ yd. each of 8 blue fabrics
¼ yd. each of 8 brown fabrics
⅛ yd. each of blue and brown for inner borders
¼ yd. each of blue and brown for outer border
2½ yds. for backing
59" x 59" square of batting
¼ yd. each of blue and brown for binding

N O T E

To achieve the gradual metamorphosis from one color to the next across the quilt, you will assemble this quilt in a different manner from others in the book. Read through, then follow each step carefully.

Directions

1. From each fabric, cut 2 strips, each 3½" wide. Construct 2 color runs using the 8 blue fabrics, and 2 color runs using the 8 brown fabrics. Construct 1 tube from the 2 blue color runs and 1 tube from the 2 brown color runs.

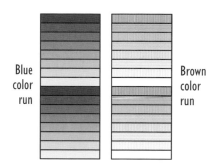

Blue color run   Brown color run

2. From the blue tube, cut the following loops:

Loop	Loop Width	Finished Width
AA1	¾"	¼"
AA2	1"	½"
AA3, AA4	1¼"	¾"

After cutting the loops from the tube, keep them folded and pin them to the design wall in order, or label them and set aside. Place safety pins in the uncut selvage end of each color-run strip from the *blue* tube. This will help keep the tubes identified as they change.

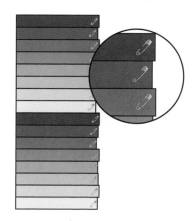

3. From the *brown* tube, cut the following loops. Pin the loops to the design wall or label as directed in step 2.

Loop #	Loop Width	Finished Width
A1, A2	2½"	2"

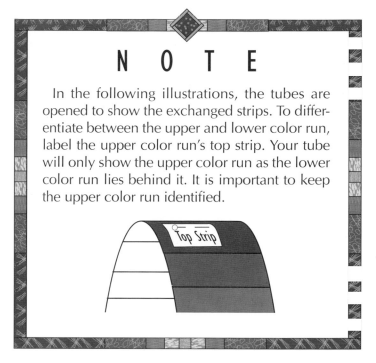

N O T E

In the following illustrations, the tubes are opened to show the exchanged strips. To differentiate between the upper and lower color run, label the upper color run's top strip. Your tube will only show the upper color run as the lower color run lies behind it. It is important to keep the upper color run identified.

4. Place the tubes side by side, with the blue tube on the left, the brown tube on the right, and the darkest value strips at the top.

Blue tube: Remove the stitching from above and below the fourth darkest color-run strip from the *upper* color run. Set the strip aside.

Brown tube: Remove the stitching from above and below the fourth darkest color-run strip from the *lower* color run and insert it in the opening in the blue tube.

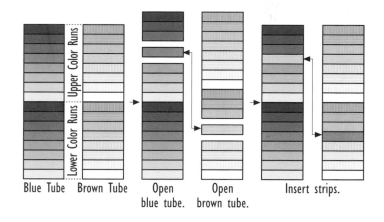

Blue Tube   Brown Tube   Open blue tube.   Open brown tube.   Insert strips.

Insert the strip removed from the blue tube into the opening in the brown tube. As you resew each strip, take care to sew accurate 1/4"-wide seams. Always remember to switch the safety pin from the blue strip to the brown strip just sewn into the blue color run.

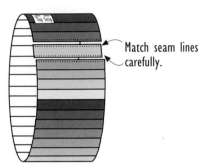

Match seam lines carefully.

5. From the resewn blue and brown tubes, cut loops referring to the chart below. Pin the loops to the design wall or label and set aside.

Loop #	Loop Width	Finished Width
Blue Tube		
BB1, BB2	1½"	1"
BB3, BB4	1¾"	1¼"
Brown Tube		
B1, B2	2¼"	1¾"

6. Remove the stitching from the following color-run strips, exchange and resew strips; switch the safety pin as you did in step 4.

Blue tube: From the *lower* color run, remove the fourth lightest strip and set aside.
Brown tube: From the *upper* color run, remove the fourth lightest strip and set aside.

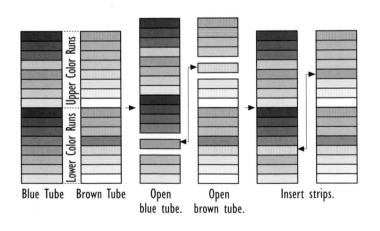

Blue Tube   Brown Tube   Open blue tube.   Open brown tube.   Insert strips.

7. From the resewn blue and brown tubes, cut loops referring to the chart below. Pin the loops to the design wall or label and set aside.

Loop #	Loop Width	Finished Width
Blue Tube		
CC1	2"	1½"
CC2	2¼"	1¾"
Brown Tube		
C1	1¼"	¾"
C2	1½"	1"
C3	1¾"	1¼"

8. Remove the stitching from the following color-run strips, exchange and resew strips; switch the safety pin as you did in step 4.

Blue tube: From the upper color run, remove the lightest strip.
Brown tube: From the lower color run, remove the lightest strip.

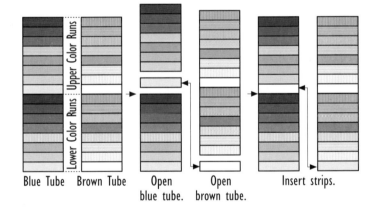

Blue Tube   Brown Tube   Open blue tube.   Open brown tube.   Insert strips.

9. From the resewn blue and brown tubes, cut loops referring to the chart below. Pin the loops to the design wall or label and set aside.

Loop #	Loop Width	Finished Width
Blue Tube		
DD1	2½"	2"
DD2	2¼"	1¾"
Brown Tube		
D1	1¼"	¾"
D2, D5	1"	½"
D3, D4	¾"	¼"

10. Remove the stitching from the following color-run strips, exchange and resew strips, and switch the safety pin as you did in step 4.

Blue tube: From the *upper* color run, remove the darkest strip.
Brown tube: From the *lower* color run, remove the darkest strip.

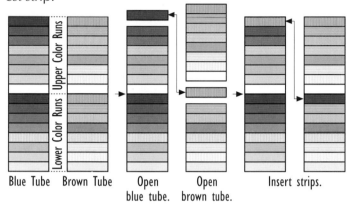

Blue Tube Brown Tube   Open blue tube.   Open brown tube.   Insert strips.

11. From the resewn blue and brown tubes, cut loops referring to the chart below. Pin the loops to the design wall or label and set aside.

Loop #	Loop Width	Finished Width
Blue Tube		
EE1	1¾"	1¼"
EE2	1¼"	¾"
EE3, EE4	¾"	¼"
Brown Tube		
E1	1¾"	1¼"
E2	1½"	1"

12. Remove the stitching from the following color-run strips, exchange and resew strips, and switch the safety pin as you did in step 4.

Blue tube: From the *lower* color run, remove the *second darkest* strip.
Brown tube: From the *upper* color run, remove the *second darkest* strip.

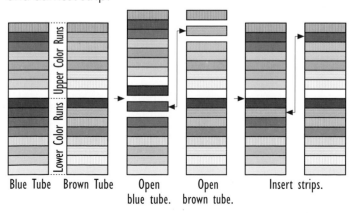

Blue Tube Brown Tube   Open blue tube.   Open brown tube.   Insert strips.

13. From the resewn blue and brown tubes, cut loops referring to the chart below. Pin the loops to the design wall or label and set aside.

Loop #	Loop Width	Finished Width
Blue Tube		
FF1	1½"	1"
FF2	2¼"	1¾"
Brown Tube		
F1	2¼"	1¾"
F2	2"	1½"

14. Remove the stitching from the following color-run strips, exchange and resew strips, and switch the safety pin as you did in step 4.

Blue tube: From the *lower* color run, remove the *third lightest* strip.
Brown tube: From the *upper* color run, remove the *third lightest* strip.

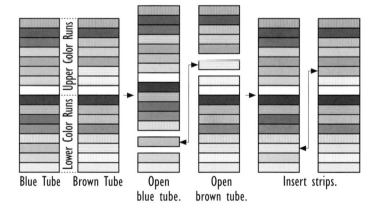

Blue Tube Brown Tube   Open blue tube.   Open brown tube.   Insert strips.

15. From the resewn blue and brown tubes, cut loops referring to the chart below. Pin the loops to the design wall or label and set aside.

Loop #	Loop Width	Finished Width
Blue Tube		
GG1	2³⁄₄"	2¹⁄₄"
Brown Tube		
G1	1"	¹⁄₂"
G2	1¹⁄₄"	³⁄₄"
G3	1³⁄₄"	1¹⁄₄"

16. Remove the stitching from the following color-run strips, exchange and resew strips, and switch the safety pin as you did in step 4.

Blue tube: From the *upper* color run, remove the *third darkest* strip.

Brown tube: From the *lower* color run, remove the *third darkest* strip.

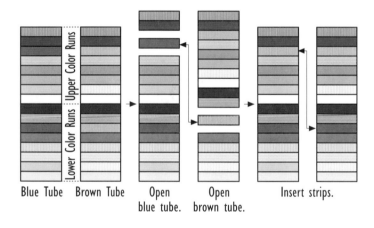

Blue Tube Brown Tube Open blue tube. Open brown tube. Insert strips.

17. From the resewn blue and brown tubes, cut loops referring to the chart below. Pin the loops to the design wall or label and set aside.

Loop #	Loop Width	Finished Width
Blue Tube		
HH1	2¹⁄₄"	1³⁄₄"
HH2	1³⁄₄"	1¹⁄₄"
Brown Tube		
H1	1¹⁄₂"	1"
H2, H3	1¹⁄₄"	³⁄₄"
H4, H5	³⁄₄"	¹⁄₄"

18. Open all the loops; alternate between pulling out seams and cutting through the top rectangle for staggered seam construction. (See directions for staggered seams in "Sewing the Bargello Strips" on pages 16–17.) Refer to the graph on page 66 for finished strip widths, placement, and direction of the curve for each opened strip. Pin Bargello strips in place on the design wall.

N O T E

If you wish to use this technique to design your own color metamorphosis, remove the same value strip from each tube but alternate the color runs. For example, if you remove the darkest strip from one tube's *upper* color run, remove the darkest strip from the other tube's *lower* color run. If you remove a strip from the first tube's *lower* color run, remove the corresponding strip from the second tube's *upper* color run.

After cutting loops from the tubes, randomly choose a new pair of strips to remove, but exchange strips in the manner directed above.

Assembling the Quilt

1. Prepare the 59" x 59" batting and backing square as directed in "Preparing the Batting and Backing" on pages 14-15.

2. Beginning with the center strip (H1), center and pin in place, right side up. Pin strip H2 on top of H1, matching right edges and staggering seams. Stitch ¹⁄₄" from the right edges. Flip strip H2 and press if necessary.

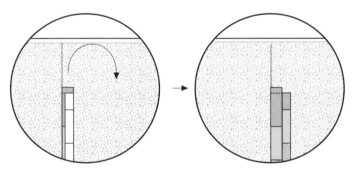

3. Continue sewing strips to the quilt, referring to "Sewing the Bargello Strips" on pages 16–19. Work across to the right side of the quilt, ending with strip A2.

4. At the quilt's center, pin strip HH2 to strip H1, matching left edges and staggering seams. Stitch, flip, and press if necessary. Continue adding strips to the quilt, working across to the left side of the quilt, ending with strip AA1.

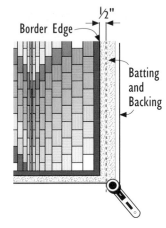
Border Edge ← ½"

Batting and Backing

Borders and Binding

1. From inner border fabric, cut 3 blue strips and 3 brown strips, each ¾" wide. Join strips as needed for side borders. Following the directions for "Borders" on pages 21-22, measure through the center of the quilt from top to bottom. Cut and sew the blue border strip to the blue side of the quilt, and the brown border strip to the brown side of the quilt.

2. For the top and the bottom borders, stitch a blue strip to a brown strip, end to end. Referring to the diagram below for suggestions, match the blue and brown sections of each border strip to the blue and brown sections of the quilt. Measure the quilt from side to side. Cut border strips, join as desired, then pin and stitch to the quilt.

4. Trim away batting and backing, leaving ½" extending beyond the edge of the outer border.

5. From binding fabric, cut 3 blue strips and 3 brown strips, each 2⅛" wide. Join ends and sew to the quilt, placing the blue strips along the blue part of the quilt, and the brown strips along the brown part of the quilt. Follow directions for single-thickness binding in "Binding" on pages 23-24. The binding will measure ¾" wide when finished.

Upper Edge

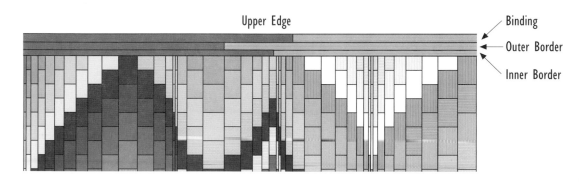

Binding
Outer Border
Inner Border

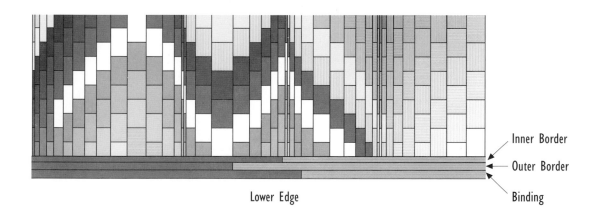

Inner Border
Outer Border
Binding

Lower Edge

3. From outer border fabric, cut 3 blue strips and 3 brown strips, each 1¼" wide. Following the directions given in steps 1 and 2 above, stitch side borders to the quilt first, then add top and bottom borders.

Fireflies

By Marge Edie, 1993, Clemson, South Carolina, 56" x 64". The background areas and the widened curve at the lower edge draw the viewer's eye around the quilt, recalling the movement of fireflies at dusk.

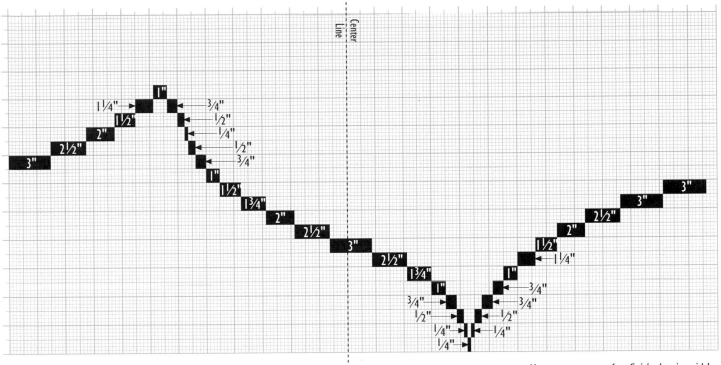

Grid squares equal ¼".

Measurements are for *finished* strip widths.

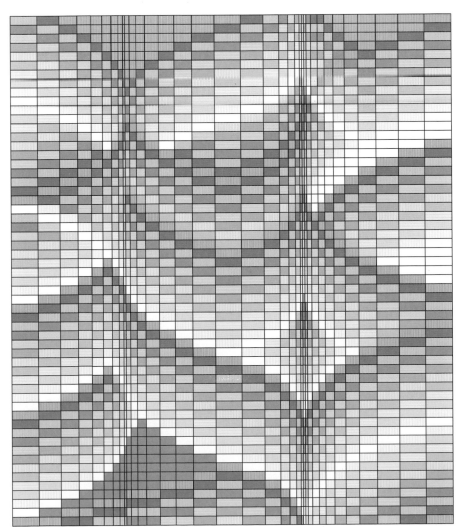

This quilt was the sample project for the first class I taught on advanced techniques. The class deadlines inspired me to cut and piece this quilt quickly! It reminds me of flitting lights in the darkness.

Materials

44"-wide fabric

⅜ yd. each of 12 colors
¼ yd. of 3 colors for background strips
¼ yd. for inner border
⅛ yd. for outer border
3½ yds. for backing
64" x 72" rectangle of batting
½ yd. for binding

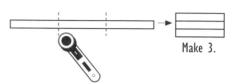

Directions

1. Cut 7 strips, each 1½" wide, from each of the 12 colors. Construct 1 color run from each set of strips to make 7 color runs. Do not sew the color runs into tubes.

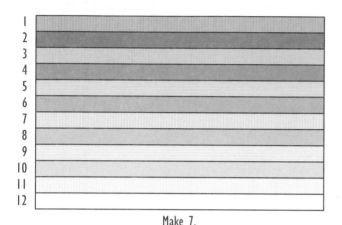

Make 7.

2. Following the graph on page 73, and the illustration in the pullout pattern insert, cut Bargello strips from color runs. Remove and/or insert rectangles as indicated on the pullout insert. Arrange and pin the Bargello strip segments to the design wall.

N O T E

The background areas in "Fireflies" on page 75 are pieced from 1½"-wide strips to repeat the horizontal seam lines across the quilt. If you wish to cut fabric rectangles without seams for the background strips, refer to the Background Sections A–E charts on the following pages. Count the number of rectangles appearing in each backround strip. Multiply the number of rectangles by 1 and add ½". Cut the backround segment to this length.

For rectangles with seams follow the directions given for segment preparation first, then refer to the charts for the order in which the background strips appear in the quilt. Referring to these charts, join or remove strip-pieced segments as needed, then, following the quilt plan on the pullout insert for placement, stitch the background strips to the Bargello strips.

Background Sections A and B

1. Cut 3 strips of background fabric, each 1½" wide. Cut each strip in thirds, then sew each group of 3 into a short strip-pieced unit.

Make 3.

2. Cut the following segments.

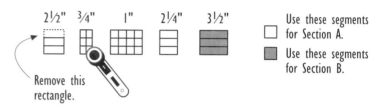

Remove this rectangle.

2½" ¾" 1" 2¼" 3½"

☐ Use these segments for Section A.
■ Use these segments for Section B.

3. Cut 2 strips of background fabric, each 1½" wide. Sew them together lengthwise to make a strip-pieced unit, then cut in half. Sew the 2 halves together to make a short 4-strip unit as shown.

Make 1.

4. Cut the following segments:

Remove these rectangles.

1¼" 1½" 1¾" 2" 2½" 3"

Remove these rectangles.

☐ Use these segments for Section A.
■ Use these segments for Section B.

5. Referring to the charts below and above right, prepare the background segments, removing or adding rectangles if needed from the segments cut in steps 2 and 4. Place them in the quilt according to the diagram in the pullout insert.

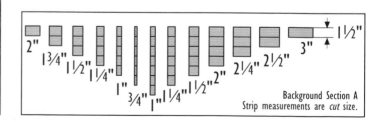

2" 1¾" 1½" 1¼" 1" ¾" 1" 1¼" 1½" 2" 2¼" 2½" 3" 1½"

Background Section A
Strip measurements are *cut* size.

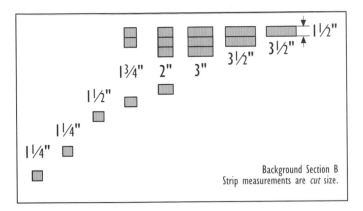

Background Section B
Strip measurements are *cut* size.

Background Sections C and D

1. Cut 2 strips of background fabric, each 1 1/2" wide. Sew them together lengthwise to make a strip-pieced unit. Cut across the strip-pieced units to make the following segments.

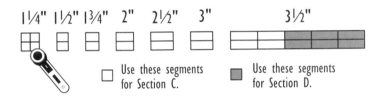

☐ Use these segments for Section C.

■ Use these segments for Section D.

2. Referring to the chart below, join strip-pieced segments if necessary, then place them in the quilt according to the quilt plan on the pullout pattern insert.

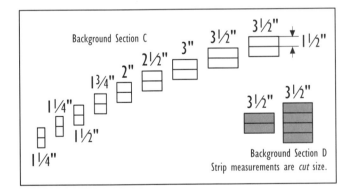

Background Section D
Strip measurements are *cut* size.

Background Section E

1. Cut 3 strips of background fabric, each 1 1/2" wide. Sew them together lengthwise to make a strip-pieced unit. Cut across the strip-pieced units to make the following segments.

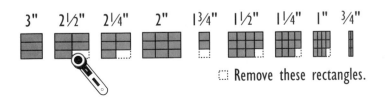

☐ **Remove these rectangles.**

2. Referring to the chart below, join or remove strip-pieced segments if necessary, then stitch the strips to the Bargello strips.

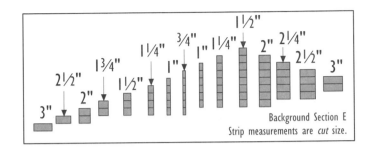

Background Section E
Strip measurements are *cut* size.

Assembling the Quilt

1. Layer backing and batting, following the directions in "Preparing the Backing and Batting" on pages 14-15.

2. Sew the Bargello strip segments you have pinned to the wall into long Bargello strips.

3. Starting at the center of the quilt, place the center strip on the prepared batting and backing. Place the next Bargello strip to the right on top of the center strip, right sides together, aligning right edges. Stitch along the strips' right edges with a 1/4"-wide seam allowance. Flip and press if necessary.

4. Continue sewing strips to the quilt, working from center to the right side. (See "Sewing the Bargello Strips" on pages 16-19.)

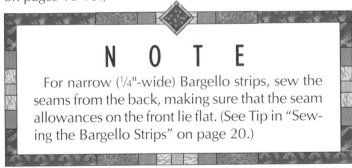

N O T E

For narrow (1/4"-wide) Bargello strips, sew the seams from the back, making sure that the seam allowances on the front lie flat. (See Tip in "Sewing the Bargello Strips" on page 20.)

5. Place the next Bargello strip to the left on top of the center strip with right sides together, aligning left edges. Stitch. Flip and press if necessary. Continue sewing strips to quilt, working from center to left side.

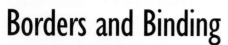

Borders and Binding

1. From inner border fabric, cut 6 strips, each 1⅝" wide. Join strips as needed. Following the directions for "Borders" on pages 21-22, sew top and bottom borders to the quilt, then add side borders.

2. From outer border fabric, cut 6 strips, each ¾" wide. Join strips, measure, cut borders, and sew to quilt as directed in step 1.

3. Trim away batting and backing, leaving about ¾" extending beyond the edge of the outer border.

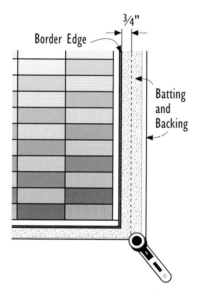

4. From binding fabric, cut 7 strips, each 2½" wide. Join ends as needed with a 45°-angle seam. Follow directions for single-thickness binding in "Binding" on pages 23–24. The binding will measure 1" wide when finished.

Mirage

By Marge Edie, 1993, Clemson, South Carolina, 34" x 47". The shimmering mirror image seems to radiate from a horizon. Separator strips create their own curve, enhancing the dimensional effect created by the bargello strips.

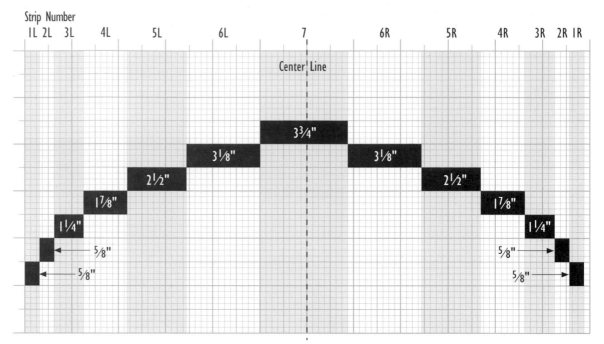

Strip Number

1L 2L 3L 4L 5L 6L 7 6R 5R 4R 3R 2R 1R

Center Line

3³⁄₄"

3¹⁄₈" 3¹⁄₈"

2¹⁄₂" 2¹⁄₂"

1⁷⁄₈" 1⁷⁄₈"

1¹⁄₄" 1¹⁄₄"

⁵⁄₈" ⁵⁄₈"

⁵⁄₈" ⁵⁄₈"

Grid squares equal ¹⁄₄".

Measurements are for *finished* strip widths.

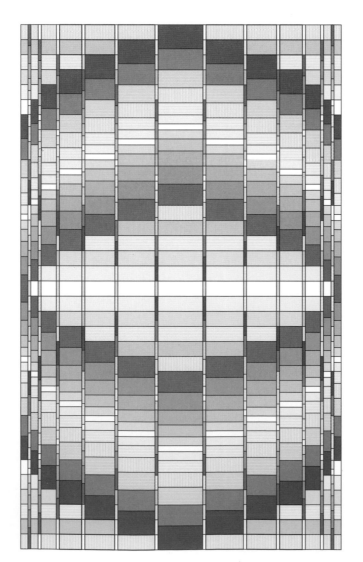

This quilt combines a mirror image of a curve with a straight-line background area at the center of the quilt. The curve will move up or down in 1¹⁄₄" steps—the finished width of the background color-run strips.

Materials

44"-wide fabric

¹⁄₄ yd. *each* of 6 dark colors
¹⁄₄ yd. *each* of 6 light colors
¹⁄₄ yd. for inner border
¹⁄₈ yd. for middle border
¹⁄₄ yd. for outer border
Scraps for corner blocks
1¹⁄₂ yds. for backing
38" x 51" rectangle of batting
³⁄₈ yd. for binding

Directions

Constructing Color Runs

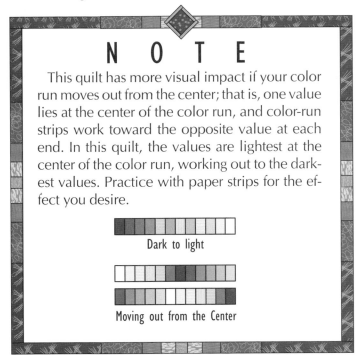

N O T E

This quilt has more visual impact if your color run moves out from the center; that is, one value lies at the center of the color run, and color-run strips work toward the opposite value at each end. In this quilt, the values are lightest at the center of the color run, working out to the darkest values. Practice with paper strips for the effect you desire.

Dark to light

Moving out from the Center

1. *Foreground color run:* Referring to the chart below, cut 2 strips from each of the fabrics. Sew each strip into a color run to make 2 "foreground" color runs. Do not sew these color runs into a tube.

Fabric #	Strip Width	Finished Width
1	2¹/₂"	2"
2, 12	2¹/₄"	1³/₄"
3, 11	2"	1¹/₂"
4, 10	1³/₄"	1¹/₄"
5, 9	1¹/₂"	1"
6, 8	1¹/₄"	³/₄"
7	1"	¹/₂"

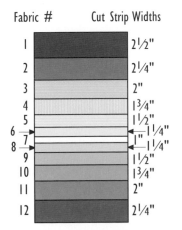

Fabric #	Cut Strip Widths
1	2¹/₂"
2	2¹/₄"
3	2"
4	1³/₄"
5	1¹/₂"
6	1¹/₄"
7	1"
8	1¹/₄"
9	1¹/₂"
10	1³/₄"
11	2"
12	2¹/₄"

2. *Background color run:* Cut 2 strips, each measuring 1³/₄" wide, from each of the 6 lightest colors (Fabrics 4–9) as shown. Construct 2 color runs from each set of 6 strips to make the "background" color runs. Do not sew these color runs into a tube.

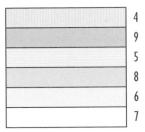

Make 2.

3. Press all the color-run seams in the same direction. (The order of the separator strips is reversed from that of the Bargello strips in the main design, so the seam allowances will automatically lie in opposite directions.)

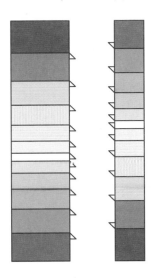

Bargello Strips

1. For each Bargello strip, cut 2 strips from the background color run, and 2 strips from the foreground color run. Refer to the graph on page 78 and the chart below for the strip widths and placement. When placing each Bargello strip, refer to the graph to see whether the curve moves up or down.

Strip # (R and L)	No. of Strips	Cut Strip Width	Finished Strip Width
1	2	$1\frac{1}{8}$"	$\frac{5}{8}$"
2	2	$1\frac{1}{8}$"	$\frac{5}{8}$"
3	2	$1\frac{3}{4}$"	$1\frac{1}{4}$"
4	2	$2\frac{3}{8}$"	$1\frac{7}{8}$"
5	2	3"	$2\frac{1}{2}$"
6	2	$3\frac{5}{8}$"	$3\frac{1}{8}$"
7	1	$4\frac{1}{4}$"	$3\frac{3}{4}$"

N O T E

Each completed Bargello and separator strip is a combination of the "background" and "foreground" color runs. Strips cut from the foreground run won't be altered as they are set into the Bargello strips.

2. For Strips 1L and R, remove and discard Fabric 12 rectangles from each foreground strip. From scraps of Fabric 12, cut 2 rectangles, each $1\frac{1}{8}$" x $2\frac{3}{4}$". For both Strips 1L and R, insert 1 of these rectangles between the foreground Bargello strips as shown.

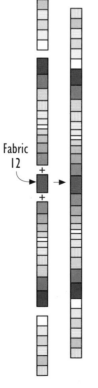

Fabric 12

3. For each remaining Bargello strip, remove rectangles from background strips and add them to foreground strips, referring to the diagrams below and on page 81. Remember to reverse the foreground strips to get a mirror image.

N O T E

Discard the duplicate rectangle of Fabric 7 when stitching each set of background color-run segments together in Bargello strips 2L & R through 7.

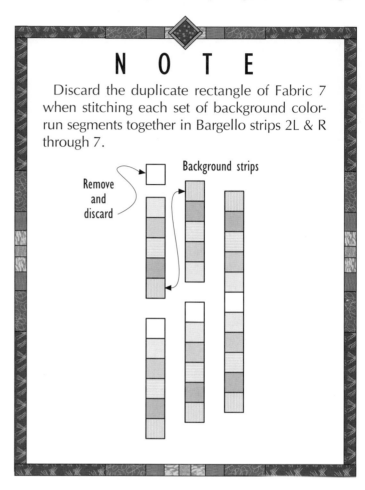

Remove and discard

Background strips

4. Arrange the completed Bargello strips on the design wall until all the strips are prepared.

Main Bargello Strips

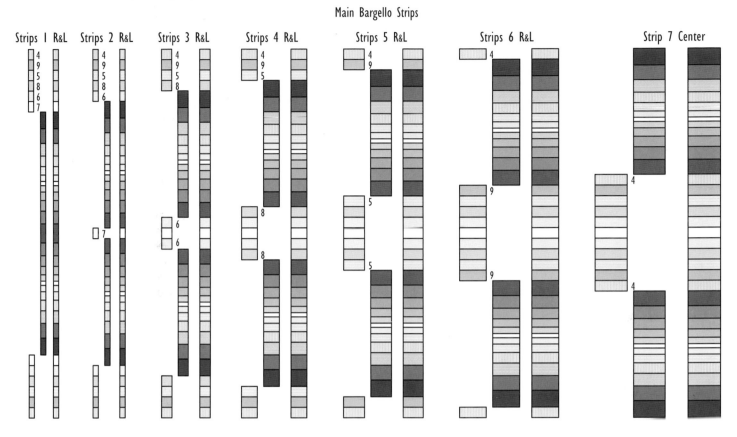

Strips 1 R&L   Strips 2 R&L   Strips 3 R&L   Strips 4 R&L   Strips 5 R&L   Strips 6 R&L   Strip 7 Center

Separator Strips

1. For each separator strip, cut 2 strips, each ¾" wide, from the foreground color run, and 2 strips, each ¾" wide, from the background color run.

2. From each pair of background color-run strips, remove and discard the duplicate rectangle of Fabric 4, then reverse one strip and stitch together as shown below.

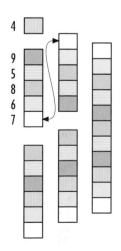

3. Sew separator strips 1L and 1R as shown. To construct separator strips 2L and 2R through 6L and 6R, remove rectangles from each background strip, then add the strip segments to the center and each end of the foreground strip as shown below.

Separator Strips

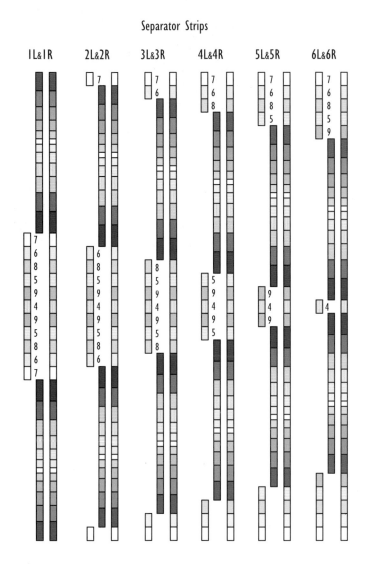

4. Alternating strips, position separator strips and Bargello strips on the design wall.

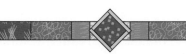

Assembling the Quilt

1. Prepare the backing and batting, following directions in "Preparing the Backing and Batting" on pages 14-15.
2. Starting at the center of the quilt, place center Strip 7 on prepared batting and backing. Place separator Strip 6R on top of Strip 7, right sides together, aligning right edges.

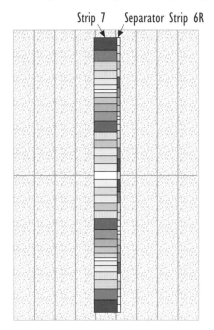

Strip 7   Separator Strip 6R

Horizontal seams match only where separator strips and background strips are side by side. (Check frequently as you work to make sure these seams line up across the quilt.) Stitch with a ¹/₄"-wide seam allowance. Flip separator Strip 6R and pin in place.

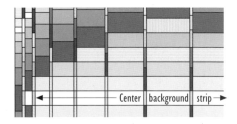

Center background strip

3. Continue sewing strips to the quilt, alternating main design strips and separator strips and working from the center to the right side.

4. Stitch separator Strip 6L to main design Strip 7 along the left edges, then continue sewing strips to the quilt, alternating separator strips with main Bargello strips and working from the center to the left side.

Borders and Binding

1. From inner border fabric, cut 5 strips, each 1½" wide. Following the directions for "Borders" on pages 21-22, measure and cut side borders. Join borders as needed to make borders long enough for your quilt. Repeat for top and bottom borders.

2. From middle border fabric, cut 5 strips, each 1" wide. Add borders, repeating step 1 above.

3. From outer border fabric, cut 5 strips, each 2" wide. Measure the quilt from top to bottom through the center and cut the side borders to this measurement.

4. Measure the quilt from side to side and cut top and bottom borders to this measurement. Sew side borders to the quilt.

5. From contrasting fabric, cut 4 squares, each 2" x 2". Sew a corner setting square to each end of the top and bottom borders, then sew the borders to the quilt.

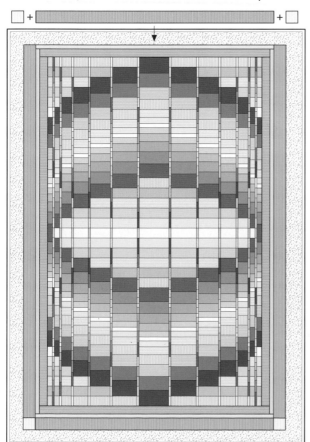

6. Trim away batting and backing, leaving about ⅞" extending beyond the edge of the outer border.

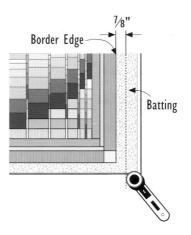

7. From binding fabric, cut 4 strips, each 2¾" wide. Sew ends together with 45°-angle seams as needed. Stitch binding to the quilt, following directions for single-thickness binding in "Binding" on pages 23-24. The binding will measure 1⅛" wide when finished.

Fractured Rhapsody

By Marge Edie, 1993, Clemson, South Carolina, 47" x 37". The rich colors in this quilt, while certainly diverse, work very well with each other. Varying values from light to dark accentuates the fractured curves, creating movement and dimension.

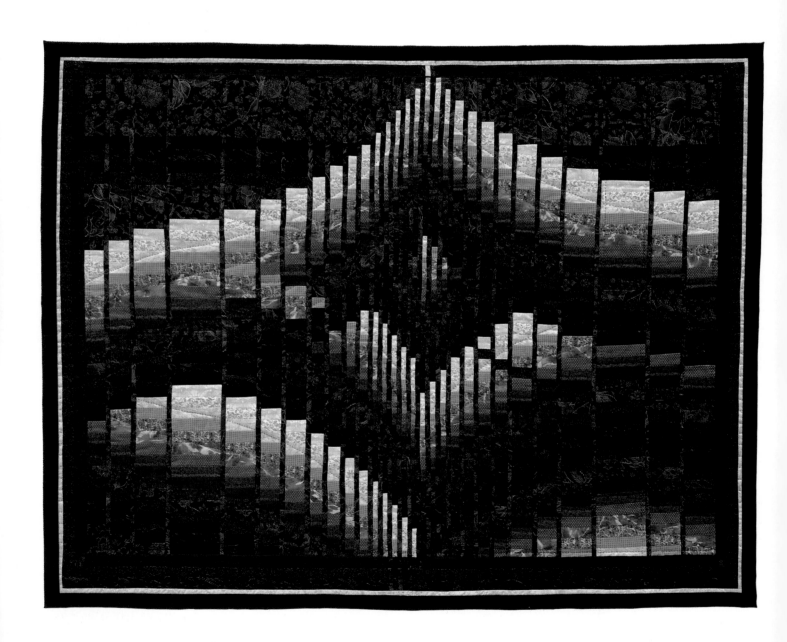

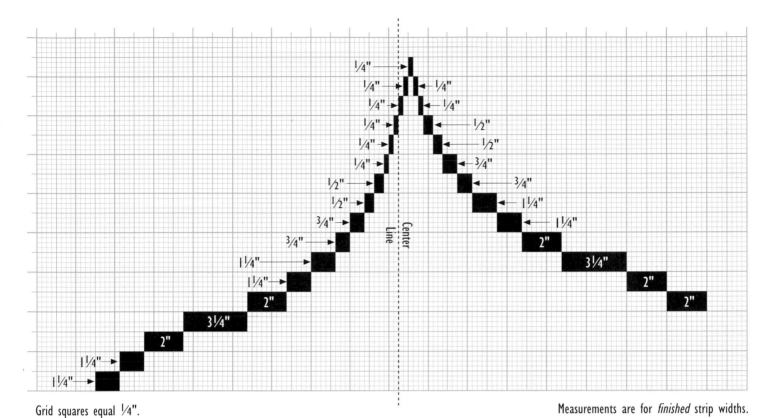

1/4"→ 1/4"
1/4"→ ←1/4"
1/4"→ ←1/4"
1/4"→ ←1/2"
1/4"→ ←1/2"
1/4"→ ←3/4"
1/2"→ ←3/4"
1/2"→ ←1 1/4"
3/4"→ ←1 1/4"
3/4"→ 2"
1 1/4"→ 3 1/4"
1 1/4"→ 2"
2" 2"
3 1/4"
2"
1 1/4"→
1 1/4"→

Center Line

Grid squares equal 1/4".

Measurements are for *finished* strip widths.

Materials

44"-wide fabric

1/4 yd. each of 14 colors
1 1/8 yds. for Fabric 11, separator
 strips, and background fabric
1/8 yd. *each* of 4 dark colors for
 background strips
1/8 yd. for 1st border
1/4 yd. *each* for 2nd and 3rd borders
1/8 yd. *each* for 4th and 5th borders
2 3/4 yds. for backing
55" x 45" rectangle of batting
3/8 yd. for binding

I began this project in a "Designing to Music" workshop with Alison Goss. I had just finished my large piece "To the Sea . . . the Coral Sea" (page 40) and was feeling a little "Bargelloed out." In order to stretch my designing skills, I decided to try "going off the curve" for the first time by removing and/or inserting Bargello segments and seeing what I could accomplish. This piece was the start of all my Bargello experiments.

I did almost no preplanning of the curve and design, playing with it a lot for about eight months. I used the separator strips to widen the design and reduce the difficulty in hand quilting caused by many bulky seams.

Directions

1. From each of the 15 colors, cut 4 strips, each 1¼" wide. From Color 12, cut 1 extra 1¼"-wide strip to use for extra pieces. Construct 1 color run from each set of strips to make 4 color runs. Do not sew them into tubes.

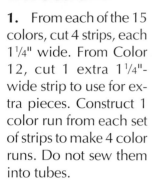

Make 4.

2. From the background fabric, cut 28 strips, each ¾" wide, for separator strips.

3. Cut 1 strip, 1¼" wide, from each of the 4 dark fabrics for background strips. Make 1 color run.

4. Cut strips from this color run, referring to the pullout insert for strip widths. Remove rectangles as necessary.

5. Referring to the charts below and above right, and the quilt plan on the pullout pattern insert, cut background fabric strips for the areas above and below the curves.

No. of Strips	Strip Width	Piece	No. of Pieces	Dimensions
1	5"	E	2	1" x 5"
		D	2	1¼" x 5"
		A	7	1¾" x 5"
		B	5	2½" x 5"
		C	2	3¾" x 5"
1	4¼"	F	1	¾" x 4¼"
		N	1	1¼" x 4¼"
		O	1	1¾" x 4¼"
1	3½"	G	1	¾" x 3½"
		M	1	1¼" x 3½"
		P	1	2½" x 3½"

No. of Strips	Strip Width	Piece	No. of Pieces	Dimensions
1	2¾"	H	1	¾" x 2¾"
		L	1	1" x 2¾"
		U	1	1¾" x 2¾"
		Q	1	2¾" x 3¾"
1	2"	I	1	¾" x 2"
		K	1	1" x 2"
		V	1	1¾" x 2"
		R	1	2" x 2½"
1	1¼"	J	2	¾" x 1¼"
		S	1	1¼" x 1¾"
		T	2	1¼" x 2½"

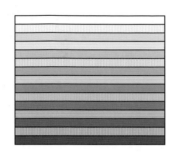

NOTE

When sewn into the quilt, backround strips cut from this cutting plan lie in the same direction as the strips you cut for the color runs. For special effects or a different print orientation, wait to cut the backround rectangles until you asssemble the quilt.

Cut the widest strip first, then cut narrower strips later from the unused portions of the strips.

6. Following the diagram on the pullout pattern insert, cut Bargello strips from the color runs made in step 1. Remove and/or insert rectangles as indicated.

Sew the dark background strips cut in step 5 to the background rectangles cut in step 4, then sew these units to the ends of the Bargello strips across the top and lower left corner of the quilt. When placing each Bargello strip, refer to the graph on page 85 to see whether the curve moves up or down.

7. Alternate assembled Bargello strips with the ¾"-wide separator strips and arrange on the design wall.

8. Prepare a 45" x 55" rectangle of backing and batting, following the directions given in "Preparing the Backing and Batting" on pages 14–15.

9. Starting at the center of the quilt, place the center strip on the prepared batting and backing. (See pages 17–18.) Place a separator strip on top, right sides together, aligning right edges. Make sure that the center of each strip matches the horizontal pencil line on the batting, and that the top and bottom ends match evenly. Stitch with a ¼"-wide seam allowance. Flip and press if necessary.

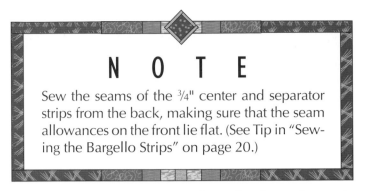

N O T E

Sew the seams of the ¾" center and separator strips from the back, making sure that the seam allowances on the front lie flat. (See Tip in "Sewing the Bargello Strips" on page 20.)

10. Continue sewing strips to the quilt, alternating main Bargello strips and separator strips and working from the center to the right side. (See "Sewing the Bargello Strips" on pages 16–21.)

11. Stitch a separator strip to the center main Bargello strip along the left edges, then continue sewing strips to the quilt, working from the center to the left side and alternating separator strips with main Bargello strips.

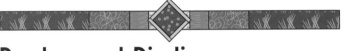

Borders and Binding

1ST *Border*

1. Cut 4 strips, each ⅝" wide. Following the directions for "Borders" on pages 21–22, measure, cut and stitch side borders to the quilt.

2. Repeat for top and bottom borders.

2ND *Border*

1. Cut 4 strips, each 1¼" wide. Measure the quilt from top to bottom through the center and cut the side borders to this measurement.

2. Pin the side borders to the quilt. From the back of the quilt, line up the 1st border's seam line with a point on the presser foot ⅛" from the needle. Sew the side borders to the quilt from the back, following the same method you used when you sewed the seams of the ¾" separator strips.

3. For the top border, sew a ¾" x 1¼" rectangle of separator fabric to each side of a ¾" x 1¼" rectangle of Fabric 1.

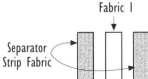

Fabric 1

Separator Strip Fabric

4. Sew a border strip to each side of the separator rectangles as shown.

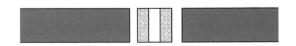

5. For the bottom border, sew a ¾" x 1¼" rectangle of separator fabric between ¾" x 1¼" rectangles of fabrics 13, 14, and 15 as shown below.

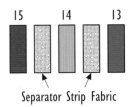

15   14   13

Separator Strip Fabric

6. Sew a ¾" x 1¼" rectangle of separator fabric to each end of the unit made in step 5, then sew a border strip to each end.

7. Measure the quilt from side to side, center the pieced border units as shown in the diagrams below, and cut top and bottom borders to this measurement.

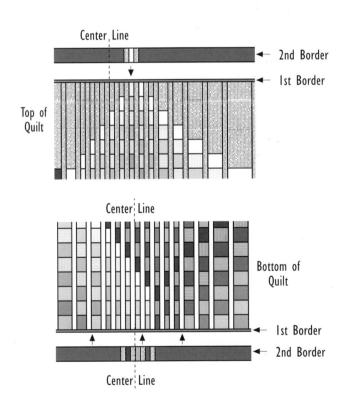

8. From contrasting fabric, cut 4 corner setting squares, each 1¼" x 1¼". Sew to each end of the border strips. Pin, then sew top and bottom borders to the quilt from the back, following the directions in step 2 for side borders.

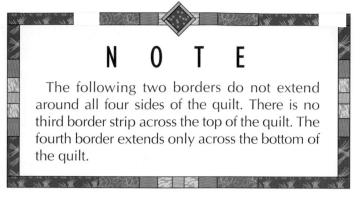

N O T E

The following two borders do not extend around all four sides of the quilt. There is no third border strip across the top of the quilt. The fourth border extends only across the bottom of the quilt.

3RD Border

1. Cut 4 strips, each 1¼" wide. Measure, cut, and sew a border strip to each side of the quilt.

2. For the bottom border strip, sew a ¾" x 1¼" rectangle of separator fabric between ¾" x 1¼" rectangles of Fabrics 13 and 14 and to each end as shown in the diagram below. Sew a border strip to each end of this unit.

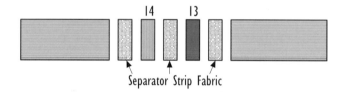

Separator Strip Fabric

3. Measure through the center of the quilt from side to side. Matching separator strip rectangles, line up the 3rd border's pieced unit with the 2nd border's pieced unit as shown below and cut the border strip to this measurement. Sew the bottom border to the quilt.

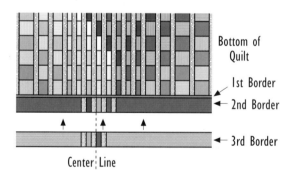

4TH Border

1. Cut 2 strips, each 1¼" wide. Sew a ¾" x 1¼" rectangle of separator fabric to each side of a ¾" x 1¼" rectangle of Fabric 13. Sew a border strip to each end.

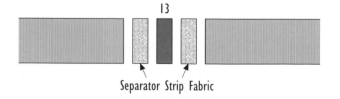

Separator Strip Fabric

2. Measure, cut, and sew the border to the bottom of the quilt, matching separator strips as shown in the diagram below left.

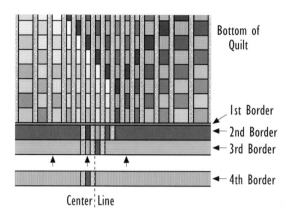

5TH Border

1. Cut 4 strips, each ¾" wide. Join ends as necessary. Measure, cut, and sew side borders to the quilt.

2. Repeat for top and bottom borders.

3. Trim away batting and backing, leaving about ¾" extending beyond the edge of the outer border.

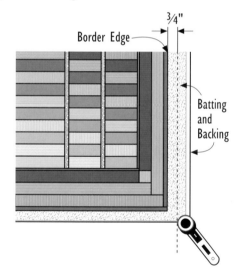

4. From binding fabric, cut 4 strips, each 2½" wide. Sew ends together with 45°-angle seams as needed. Bind, following directions for single-thickness binding in "Binding" on pages 23-24. Be careful to maintain the ¼" outer border width all the way around the quilt. The binding will measure 1" wide when finished.

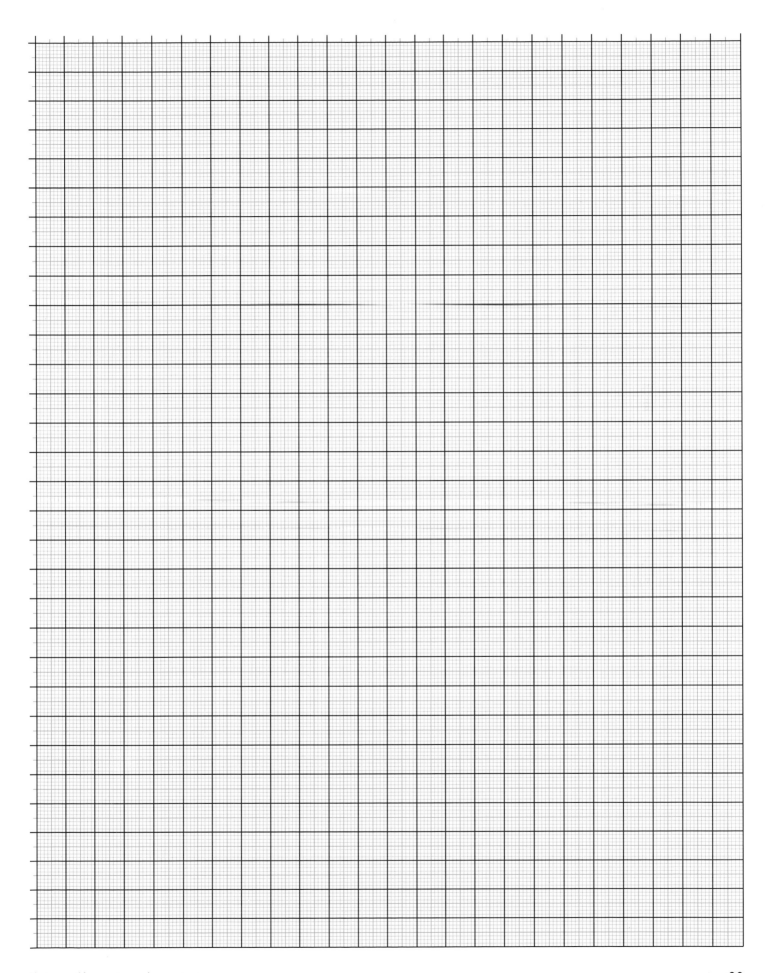

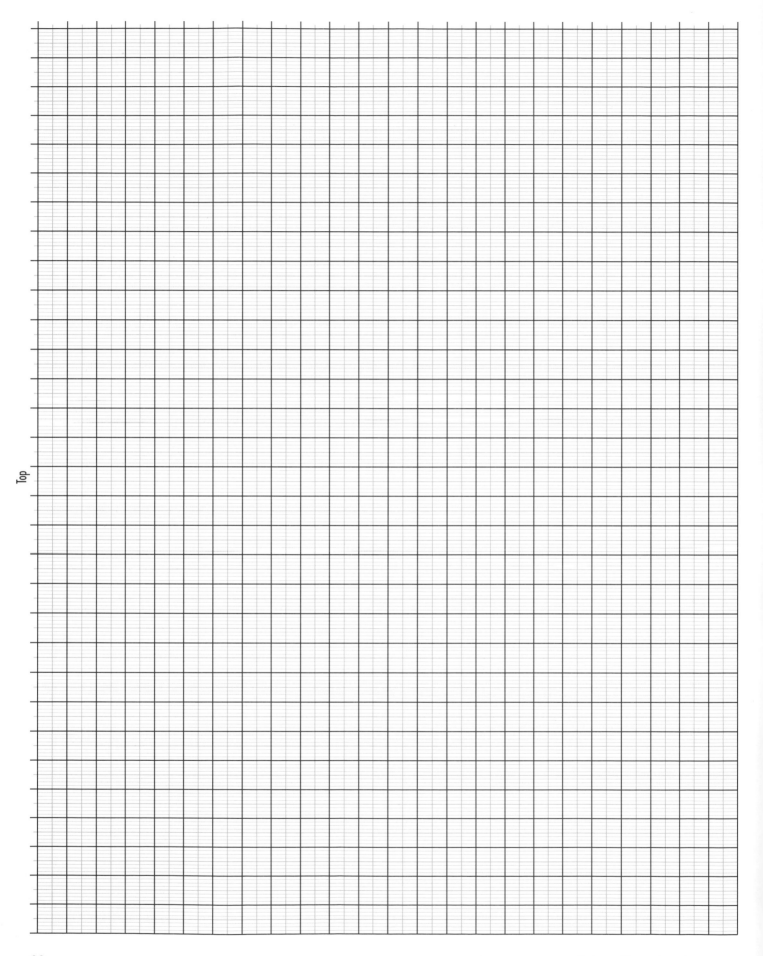

Top

Photocopy this page to graph your curves.

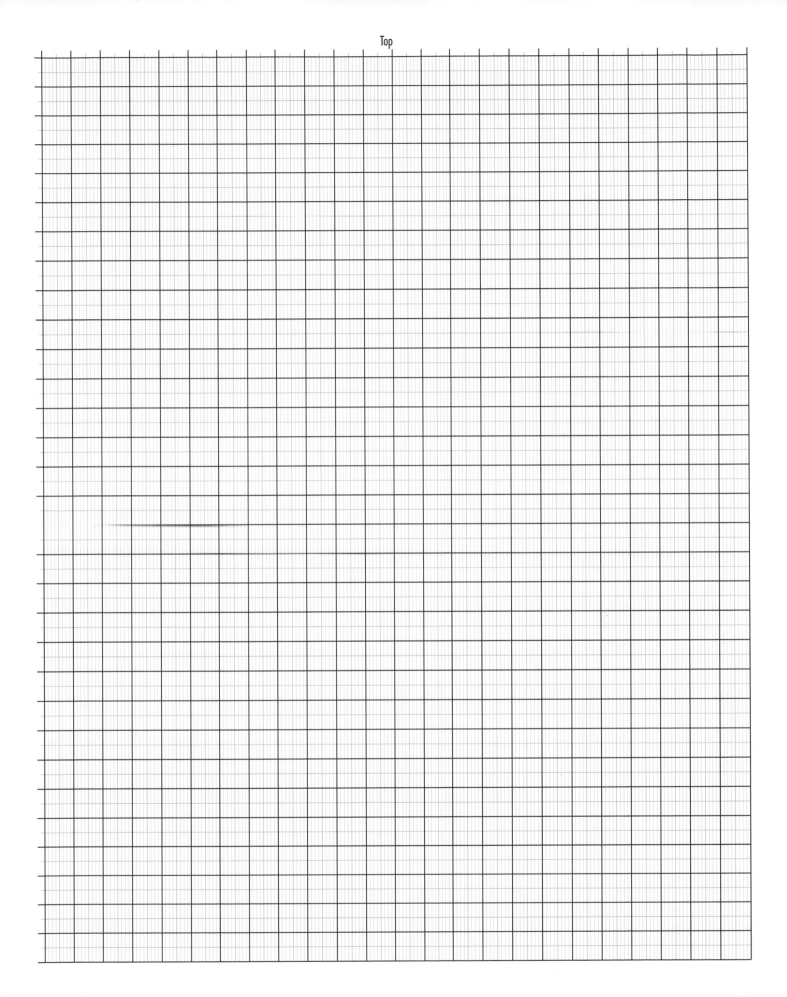

Photocopy this page to graph your curves.

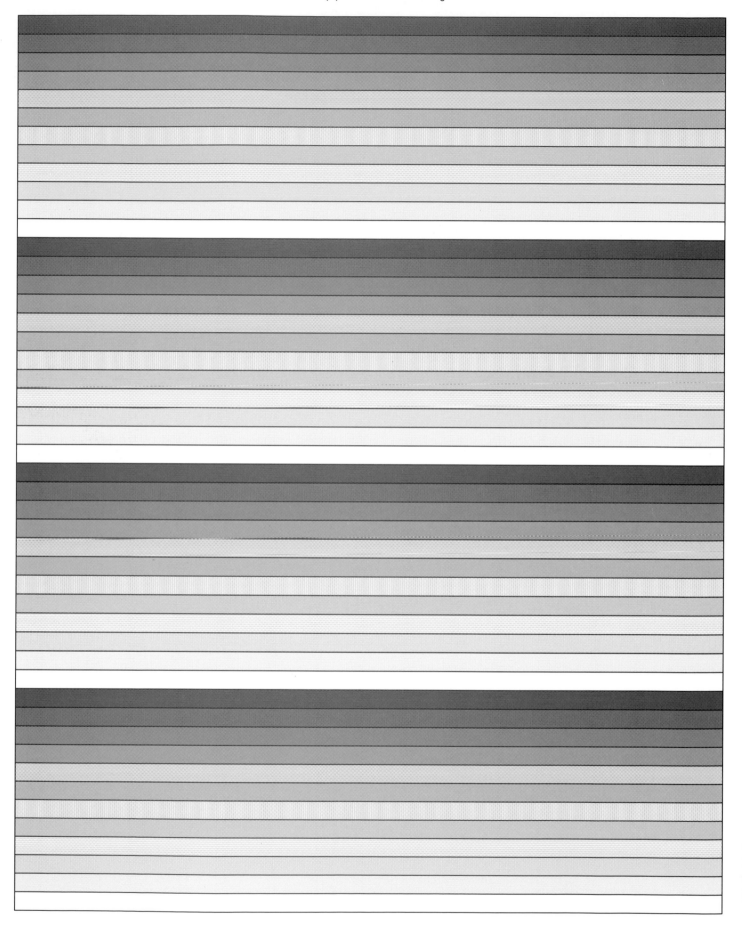

Photocopy this page to cut Bargello strips.

Photocopy this page to cut Bargello strips.

Photocopy this page to cut Bargello strips.

Publications and Products

Many titles are available at your local quilt shop.
For more information, write for a free color catalog
to That Patchwork Place, Inc., PO Box 118, Bothell,
WA 98041-0118 USA.

☎ U.S. and Canada, call **1-800-426-3126** for the
name and location of the quilt shop nearest you.
Int'l: 1-206-483-3313   Fax: 1-206-486-7596
E-mail: info@patchwork.com
Web: www.patchwork.com   3.97